Bellamy's Europe

To

Rufus

Henrietta

Brighid

Eoghain

Bellamy's Europe
David Bellamy

British Broadcasting Corporation

The programmes were first broadcast on BBC-1 on
Thursdays at 6.50 pm beginning 8th July, 1976

Produced by Mike Weatherley

Published to accompany a series of programmes prepared in
consultation with the BBC Further Education Advisory Council

Published by the
British Broadcasting Corporation
35 Marylebone High Street
London W1M 4AA

ISBN 0 563 16066 7

First published 1976
© David Bellamy 1976

Printed in England
by Butler and Tanner Ltd, Frome, Somerset

This book was set in Monophoto Melior 720
by Art Reprographic (London) Ltd, London EC1

Contents

Preface

This book is the permanent record of the ten ephemeral television programmes which inspired it and which were, in their turn, the result of four years of thought and discussion. In planning the series, we decided to forgo a systematic approach in favour of selecting areas of Europe where David Bellamy had a special knowledge and which allowed that essential ingredient for a television programme – a good story. However, we have managed to encompass most of the main vegetation zones of our continent and have endeavoured to show why they are worthy of our attention, concern and protection.

I record my gratitude to the many technicians and production staff who made the series possible and to my friend and collaborator David Bellamy for allowing the preparation of this work to be so enjoyable.

Mike Weatherley
Producer
Bellamy's Europe

Introduction

Autumn is the best time for planning and, as the clocks go back, I like to settle down with my extra hour, draw up *Walters' Climate Atlas of the World* and plan my holidays. Next year, I'm for Europe and, now that we are a part of it, a continental holiday has an almost parochial touch; but what a parish!

Outside, it's cold and wet, so naturally my eyes flick across the pages which promise warmth without the promise of rain.

One of Europe's Driest Spots, day or night, is the Cabo de Gata. Europe's High Spot is Mont Blanc, all 4807 metres of it and although there isn't a meteorological station on top, it must have a climate to match.

Fig 1(a) *Desertscape near the Cabo da Gata*

Fig 1(b) *Mont Blanc, cold summit of the EEC*

What is it going to be: the beach, the piste, a car through the karst, a 'steppe' through eastern Russia, a cheap day to Calais or a 'corker' in the Caucasus? Whatever your whim, it's all there waiting, just 21 miles across La Manche – to you and me the ever-so-English Channel.

The funny thing is that, some 8000 years ago, the Channel wasn't there, or rather the Channel was but it was empty, devoid of any salt water. The Channel was as dry as the proverbial Cabo da Gata and the British Isles a mere peninsula – an extension of the mother land mass.

As the ice sheets of the last glacial epoch began to melt (and, let's get it straight, that is exactly what they did, melt where they were; they did not withdraw, as many textbooks might lead you to believe), they left a bare landscape, devoid of life but brimfull of opportunity; so much so that the plants and animals which had spent a long winter holiday, (something under a million years) down in the warm south, began slowly to migrate northwards to clothe the new landscapes with a mantle of living green.

As the ice melted, the water so released flowed down the rivers to the seas, slowly topping them up – and thereby hangs my first tale.

The only problem is that I was never much good at French. In my schooldays there were no language laboratories – just je suis, tu es, il est; so I well remember how relieved I was on my first trip across the Channel to find that all the notices on the quayside were in English. 'Moules and chips avec tea', not even a 'Pomme de terre' in sight. I was in! It was for this reason that I wanted to call the programme **Oh La La and Chips.** However, with due deference to family viewing, I agreed to **Vive La Difference,** which I must admit is much more appropriate; for this is all about just that, the real live differences between the two sides of the English Channel. From the moment during some idyllic summer about 5500 BC, when the rising water broke through to encircle and insulate the British Isles, the Channel has acted as a challenge to all pontificators intent on making their way across the face of Europe.

Or so it was until 25th August 1875, when Captain Matthew Webb, with no external aid save a regulation bathing dress, proved that the Channel could be swum; thus re-linking us biologically with France.

Leaving the White Cliffs of Dover, one sets out in the full knowledge that the chalk which forms those white bastions of Britain, is not all that far beneath one's splashing feet.

Much of the Straits of Dover is very shallow and it is possible to stop in mid-swim, duck-dive and touch the bottom. All you need is the faith that you can do it, backed by a lot of practice at holding your breath while actively swimming. It is well worth the effort, for there is the chalk under a layer of grey ooze gaudily bedecked with all sorts of canned artefacts. There, too, a strange sight can meet your eyes, a slowly moving mass of small fish fingerling their way along. They are young herring, for this is one of the herring's favourite nursery grounds.

This is not the place to be when a super-tanker goes through, especially if it's low tide, because then there can be only just sufficient depth of water to allow them to pass. You do not even have to be there, the evidence is clear in the churned-up silts, and one can only guess how many herring have ended their day with an 'all screwed up' sensation in their lateral lines.

Breath-hold diving to depths in excess of ten metres is fraught with one main problem and that is lack of time on the bottom and, as you can see, the bottom of the Channel can be a very interesting place. I well advise a trip by aqualung, visibility can be excellent, so much so that you can sit in the ooze, see your boats bobbing about 20 metres away on the surface and view the choicest bric-a-brac, stretching away into the milky, golden brown middle distance, and back into the recent history of man's channel crossing endeavours.

The golden brown colour is due to the predominance of golden brown pigments produced by the plant plankton in the water. German oceanographers have a much more emotive word for it – *gelbstoff* – and it produces a very different picture from the blue which typifies all underwater scenes in warmer climes. As for the bric-a-brac, well my best haul to date was a gaggle of ultra modern ring-pull cans, each torn in half as a manifestation of manhood, assorted bits and pieces of crockery, one marked 'S.R.', a small shell case circa 1918, three Victorian type marmalade jars and the neck of a 'pop alley' bottle with a sea anemone attached. A word of warning – if you do take to mid Channel, remember to fly your diving flag!

Meanwhile, back to the Channel swim; 33kms (21 miles) is not all that far and, as long as the current is not adverse, it can be done in a mere 9 hours 35 minutes, proven by Barry Watson and, a little later, by a lady, Lynne Cox who took just a little longer, 9 hours 36 minutes – Oh, Equality!

Today there are many ways of getting across, some being more exalted than others, from boat through 'hover' to plane; you can choose for yourself but, for the majority the port of entry is Boulogne, with Dieppe running a close second.

Whichever way you come, as soon as you clap eyes off the sea you know that you are not in England. No, it's not just the notices, nor is it the berets and strings of onions, (in fact, I have seen more of both of these in Chelsea). It's! It's? It's different and that difference is plastered all over the landscape.

Vive La Différence

(Well, they do it in films, so why not have the title in the middle of a chapter?)

That difference is very surprising because, whichever port you or the prevailing weather conditions have selected, you end up in the Pas de Calais which is a mirror image of the Kentish landscape you have so recently left behind.

When the Alps were in the process of formation, the area of chalk which includes the famous White Cliffs, was pushed up to form a gigantic dome of soft eminently erodable rock. In time the highest parts of the dome were eroded away to reveal the older rocks beneath which now outcrop as a more or less orderly series in the following order. Chalk, Gault Clay, Lower Greensand, and Wealden Clay. On the English side the North and South Downs form the outer ring of chalk and

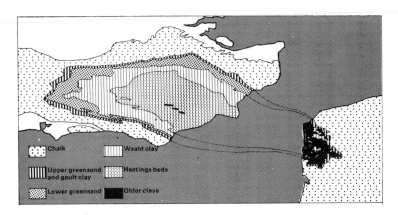

Fig 2 *Rock around the Channel*

the soft clay centre with its central ridge of sandstone in the Weald of Kent. On the French side, the clay centre is called the Boulonnais and that is ringed in much the same way by Lower Greensand, Gault and Chalk. There are differences, for example the clays of the Boulonnais are older than those of the Weald but there is no getting away from the fact that the two landscapes are in fact mirror images of each other even though the mirror is of a distorting nature: one other main feature of difference is that the long escarpment slopes of the North Downs face predominantly south, whereas the main escarpments on the French side face north: and that makes for a big difference in their microclimate. You can check it up for yourselves by simply comparing the North and South Downs.

Next time you look over the White Cliffs of Dover, take note, there is a lot of green about; now compare them with the more aptly named cliffs of Cap Blanc Nez – they are shining white.

Fig 3 *The green cliffs of Dover*

Fig 4 *The white cliffs of Cap Blanc Nez*

Someone's mother isn't using . . .

So why is this? The fact is that these French cliffs face straight into the teeth of all up channel weather and, facing predominately north, they never get the hot direct rays of the sun. So, many of the French cliffs are nasty cold places on which to make a home. Add to this the fact that, unprotected, they are always being eroded, baring new chalk and there's the answer. Dover's cliffs are, in part, protected from the onslaught of the waves and are thus eroding at a much slower rate and on their warm, south facing slumps a luxuriant vegetation can develop.

The green cliffs of Dover are partly covered by dense stands of Privet and Bramble, with southern plants like Stinking Iris, Golden Samphire and the clinging Wild Madder, a close relative of the Bedstraws. In late summer the bases of even the whitest parts turn a delicate blue as the Rock Sea Lavender comes into flower. In contrast, the French cliffs are devoid of just about everything except patches of the hardy Sea Cabbage.

Botanists with a day return ticket, do not be dismayed! Whatever the onshore wind doesn't do for the cliffs, it does for the sand dunes. Any itinerant plant hunter swimming the Channel is in for a shock. The first plant he meets will, more often than not, be Marram Grass just like home but, once over the first dune ridge it's unbelievable. Rolling dunes stretching away down coast as far as the eye can see, their ridges and hollows a riot of impenetrable scrub – Privet and the most prickly of coastal defenders the Sea Buckthorn, with the damper spots marked by stands of the Common Reed, crew-cut by the wind. If you want to see the like in Britain, then head for the coast of Lincolnshire for, in comparison, the dunes around Dover are 'psammateurs'.

If you are ever on holiday in the Pas de Calais, then head south of Boulogne (where you should stop to sample Les Moules Marinières), south of Bagatelle (where you should stop to leave the non botanical part of the family at the fabulous amusement park), then a sharp turn left takes you to a wonderland of dunes.

Here the dunes are large enough to have among their ridges large, water filled slacks around which a rich wetland flora is to be found. Here, if you are very lucky, you may find the delicate Fen Orchid. This orchid is today a great rarity in Britain, growing only in one or two very secret spots; so too over much of Europe its wetland habitats are being destroyed and we are in danger of losing this delicate plant. Here, in the Pas de Calais it still has a number of strongholds and here lies one of the great differences between the French and English scene.

The French side has a lot more wetlands still in an undrained state. I am afraid that the reason is not one of conservation, neither is it a sign of poor land use for which French farmers are unfairly accused; it is a manifestation of the great French hunting instinct. Take, for instance, the fact that during an average year, the towns spew out enough 'sportsmen' armed with the best in modern lead-shot shooters and they alone slaughter an estimated five million birds.

No, I am not against wildfowling, I can't be, because I enjoy roast duck, but there must be a limit. Take for example duck decoys, I always reckoned that they were a bit unsporting but, when the decoys consist of flocks of tethered live ducks then I feel that it should be stopped.

So, I am afraid that many of these wetland areas are rather pitiful places, but there is no getting away from the fact that they are full of interest and of surprises, not the least being the variety of Amphibians that may be found; here there is a very real difference compared with the English side.

Fig 5 *An Edible Frog in the hand*

Rana esculenta, as its name suggests is edible, or rather it has very edible legs joined to a not so edible croaking end. Resplendent with a yellow-green line down its back, it blends into the floating weed but, unfortunately gives itself away by raucous croaking which attracts all would-be frog snatchers in the vicinity.

Standing in the dune slacks of the Pas de·Calais it is an interesting thought that some time in the past, as the post ice age weather was warming up, all the Amphibians – Frogs, Toads, Newts and Salamanders came hopping and crawling their way northwards.

The Common Frog, Toad, Natterjack and three sorts of Newts made it to England before the Channel filled up. A lot more either got across and then later died out, or they reached the ponds of the French coast too late. Faced with a salty barrier, which is death to a delicate skinned Amphibian, they stayed put and continued to croak in French. If it is as difficult for a French frog to croak in English as it is for someone whose native language is English to say 'Grenouille', which is frog in French, then I don't blame them. The interesting fact is that a number of attempts to introduce a whole range of the Continental amphibians to Britain have met with but limited success. The main reason appears to be that in British waters very few of the tadpoles reach metamorphosis (that is few manage to turn into frogs), as compared to the 'all change' rate back in their homeland. It could be that the English climate just doesn't suit them and/or it could be competition with the ones that are already present. All those English frogs grumbling about the limited diet of English insects could well put off the fastidious French visitors.

Climatically, there is a difference; and that is why we Britons, ancient or otherwise, head south for the warmth of summer or the 'coolth' of winter frosts. Our oceanic climate, with its warm wet summers and cool wet winters, is not one of extremes. In contrast, the climate of the Central Continent is very extreme with hot summers and very cold winters.

The cold-blooded Amphibians are not quite as adaptable as the Mammals and although they can hibernate throughout the continental winter, they do need a nice summer, one that is long enough and hot enough to allow them to warm up, get croaking, eat enough and reproduce. Not only the Amphibians but all cold-blooded animals are limited in this respect, and none more so than the Reptiles.

The Common Lizard, *Lacerta vivipara*, as its second name suggests, does not lay eggs; the eggs are retained inside the mother, where they develop and hatch, the baby lizards are then 'laid' all raring to go! This Lizard is said to be Oviparous, a feature shared with the Adder and the Slow Worm, all of which are found throughout England and Scotland. In contrast, the Sand Lizard and Grass Snake lay eggs, which need the warmth of the sun for hatching, and these two reptiles are confined to England and are most abundant in the warm south.

Fig 6 *The Amphibia of North West Europe (Opposite page)*

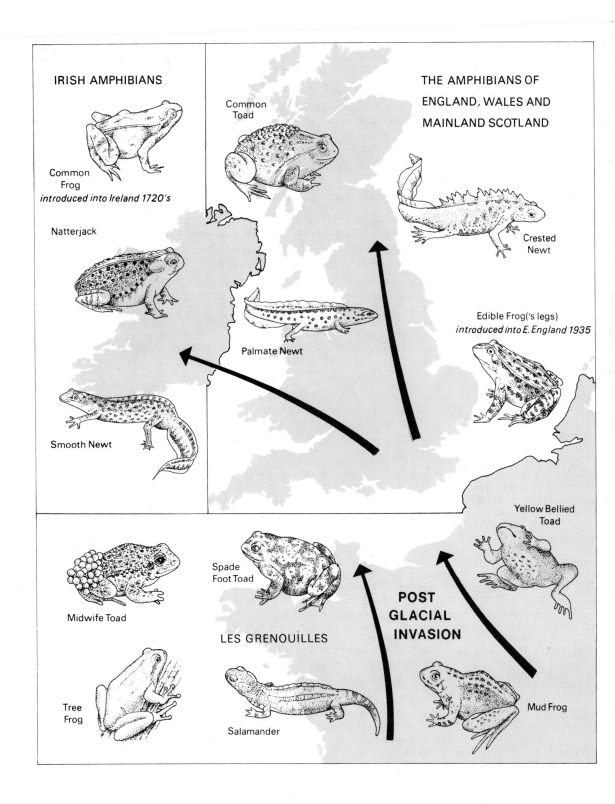

IRISH AMPHIBIANS

Common
Frog
introduced into Ireland 1720's

Natterjack

Smooth Newt

Common
Toad

**THE AMPHIBIANS OF
ENGLAND, WALES AND
MAINLAND SCOTLAND**

Palmate Newt

Crested
Newt

Edible Frog('s legs)
introduced into E. England 1935

Midwife Toad

Tree
Frog

Spade
Foot Toad

LES GRENOUILLES

Salamander

**POST
GLACIAL
INVASION**

Yellow Bellied
Toad

Mud Frog

Once south of the Channel, the numbers of Amphibians and Reptiles increase dramatically. The reason is, probably, a mixture of climate and the fact that the salty barrier has been in place for more than 7,500 years.

There is, however, a set of differences which would be difficult to explain on climatic grounds, and that is the undoubted fact that certain Mammals appear never to have made the crossing.

Mammals, except those down under, do not lay eggs; so there should be no climatic problem, except perhaps for the very tiny ones which lose their body heat very rapidly. Similarly, all of them must surely be able to move and hence migrate faster than their hopping colleagues. So, why didn't the Bicoloured and White Toothed Shrews, the Garden Dormouse, the Pine and Common Vole and the Beech Marten make it to Britain?

Fig 7 Beech Marten

The reason could well be that many of these animals are very dependent on the habitat in which they live – and their habitats are certain types of vegetation. There is, therefore, every likelihood that they had to wait and migrate with their vegetation type; that means they had to wait until all the plants which go to make up their habitat had gone before and become established; only then could they follow along.

The Amphibians were more lucky in this respect, their requirements were relatively simple, all they needed were ice free pools of water with aquatic plants and a surfeit of insect food. The melting ice produced pools galore, ponding the way to the Channel and beyond.

Many Mammals got there in time, but it would appear that at least six arrived at the Channel ports too late to make the crossing.

We have more recently obtained proof as to the effectiveness of the Channel and, indeed, of much narrower bodies of salt water as a barrier to the migration of mammals. Grey Squirrels were introduced into Britain in the 1870's. Since that time they have spread, taking over the south of England. To date, they have not crossed over to the Isle of Wight, let alone across to France, despite all the cross Channel traffic.

So it looks as if it is safe to conclude that the Channel is a barrier to the migration of land animals, except for Captain Webb and his brigade of swimmers, which is growing year by year.

How about the plants? What about all those wind- and water-borne seeds and all the others that so readily stick on feathers, fur and passing feet? Surely a mere 33 km would not act as an effective barrier to them?

Well, here we are very lucky because one of Britain's best and most active field botanists, Dr Francis Rose has been hard at work, checking the facts. For a long time he lived in Kent and he found the Channel no barrier to his botanical wanderings. Working in close association with Professor J. M. Géhu of Lille, he gathered the data and recorded it in great detail in a series of fascinating papers.

He concluded that, although there is a difference between the flora of the two sides, most of them can be explained away on grounds of differing geology, topography and land use. In fact, it looks as if there are only six Flowering Plants which could be reckoned to have remained stuck on the French side.

PLANTS WHICH REACHED THE FRENCH COAST
PERHAPS TOO LATE, THEY DIDN'T GET ACROSS

Latin Name	Anglicised Name	Probable Method of Seed Dispersal
Cirsium oleraceum	Yellow Thistle	Wind
Veronica teucrium	Blue Speedwell	Animal
Senecio spathulifolium	Spathulate Ragwort	Wind
Myosotis arenaria	Sand Forget-me-not	Animal
Orchis palustris	Water Orchis	Wind
Carex trinervis	Three-nerved Sedge	Animal

Fig 8 *The Yellow Thistle says welcome to France*

Of these, only the first one can be spoken of as common and widespread; and it is the plant that always welcomes me to the Continent. Its large sulphur-yellow flower heads, usually covered with bees and visited by butterflies, grace the wet roadside ditches leading you on to the Continent. Even when the flowers are gone, the leaves which come in two distinct shapes and a range of intermediates give the game away. It is, however, difficult to see why it didn't move on, because the handsome flower heads produce a great mass of seeds, each with a silken parachute, ideal for channel hopping. The same goes for the other five; there seems no valid reason why they couldn't get across – perhaps they are just bad sailors!

Of all the plants found on the coast of the Pas de Calais, the Yellow Thistle should be a native member of the British flora. It isn't – and repeated attempts at introducing it have met with only limited success. There are colonies at a number of places, including some in Scotland, but they seem to stay put. Is it climate, or is it competition with all those well established English, Scottish and Welsh Thistles which are already ruling its chosen habitat – a case of rank racial discrimination?

So plant-wise, there appears to be but little real natural difference between the maritime fringes of the two sides, and so it looks as if the Straits of Dover never was an important barrier to the migration of plants.

Having said that, it has reminded me of one very striking difference between the flora of the two coasts. A holiday in France will guarantee sand for your sandwiches without the pain of a pebble-dashed backside! The Pas de Calais cannot boast, (as if it would want to!), of shingle beaches and, in the absence of shingle, the very handsome Sea Pea cannot grow. In the past it was found in just one French spot, from which it has long since gone; it is, however, still abundant in several places on the English coast and appears to be spreading.

Next time you are in the environs of Dover waiting for a boat, hover around the shingle banks and see this handsome plant but, remember to leave it there for other visitors to enjoy. Also, while you are waiting, nip along to the churchyard at Ringwould in Kent and look at the gigantic Yew trees from which (or so a parishioner told me) were cut the longbows used at Agincourt. Looking at the size of the trees, I can well believe it.

It is not only in the churchyards but also in some of the local woodlands that you can see the dark, rather mysterious foliage of *Taxus baccata*, raw material for the best of British longbows. Take a real close look. The bright red 'berries' are not berries at all, the proper name for them is an Aril, for the Yew is a conifer, not a flowering plant. In the same way, take your last look for, once across the Channel you won't see another Yew until you are south of the Seine or west of the Meuse.

The farmers of the Pas de Calais have removed them from their fabulous piece of land, perhaps in remembrance of Agincourt but more probably on account of their poisonous leaves.

Another Kentish friend that is sadly very rare in the copses of the Boulonnais is our common Primrose. Mind you, if we do not stop digging it up from the wealden woodlands, a day trip to France will be even more like staying at home!

So there are differences – due to climate, habitat, land-use, custom and due to those 35 km of water, which can be so rough. So every time I board the boat on my way home, complete with regulation bottles and a string of onions, I shout **'Vive La Différence'** in my best Cockney accent, of course.

Mezzanine

If Fortnum and Mason's can have a Mezzanine floor, I don't see why a book cannot follow suit with a mezzanine chapter and, as the next bit is not strictly covered by any one of the programmes or chapters and yet is of relevance to them all, I felt I should put it here.

A day trip to Calais, with its glimpse of plants and animals yet to come, is sufficient to give anyone a dose of the wanderlust so, before we get carried even further away, perhaps we should get our feet more firmly on the background of facts.

Whenever I set out on my travels, I always take the appropriate flora and now, thanks to Professor Vernon Hayward *et al*, (and the *al* refers to a whole group of his learned botanical colleagues), there can be no excuse. We have the Flora Europaea. Don't be put off by the title, apart from the title and the proper names of the plants, the bulk of it is in English. Only one word of warning; the bulk of it is way beyond most airlines' definition of light reading material! Second on my packing list are maps, and some of the cheap ones produced by the petrol companies are ideal, both for planning your routes and marking your finds for future reference.

My first map shows, very roughly, the maximum extent of

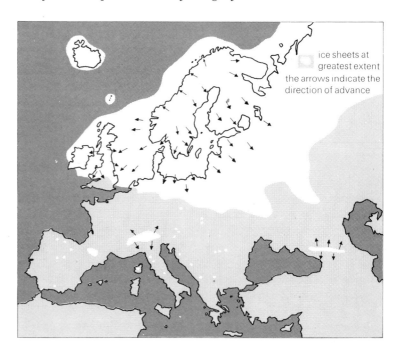

ice sheets at greatest extent the arrows indicate the direction of advance

Fig 9 *Europe under ice*

the ice sheets of the last glacial epoch. Yes! All that was covered with ice and, although your great granny won't remember it, in biological terms it wasn't all that long ago. All that terrain was deep frozen. The great weight and ponderous movements of the ice eroded and ground down the rocks, preparing the landscape for the post-glacial spring to come.

The second map attempts to summarise the present day situation climatewise, conveniently dividing the face of Europe into eight zones. Each of these zones has, or rather had, before man started mucking about with them, its own particular types of vegetation.

The main difficulty of trying to deal with these zones is to know exactly where to start! Should it be in the 'appy 'oliday zone of the Mediterranean, working north to the Arctic Tundra, or should the starting point be in 'les parapluies' country much nearer home, stepping out the other way towards the mysteries of the East?

In the end, I decided to follow a somewhat illogical pattern, radiating out from the heights of the Dolomites, north, south, east and west, to end up in one small corner of Southern Italy.

Coming down the mountains sets the picture of the highland climate. It is, in fact, quite an appropriate place in which to start because, of all the landscape features, it is the mountains which really 'muck up' the climatic zones of Europe. They stick up in various places like cold thumbs, producing rain traps and shadows. The further up their peaks one goes, the closer does the climate approximate, at least temperature wise, to the arctic. The main difference is that in the true arctic the summer days are very long, some of them being continuous, and likewise in winter the sun never rises. It's funny how we all like to dash off up north to rave about the midnight sun, but never do the same about midday darkness. Nevertheless, the low growing plants, even in the southern Alps may well experience total darkness for several of the winter months as they will be covered with a thick blanket of snow.

So, in the mountains, the type of vegetation will be, in the main, dependent on altitude. A ride up in a cable car can be, both vegetationally and environmentally, like a trip from the south of France to the Arctic Circle. The further north the mountains are situated, the worse will be the overall climate of each altitudinal zone and so, in the Pyrenees and the southern Alps the limit of tree growth is around the 1,500-1,800 metre mark; whereas along the Arctic Ocean it is at sea level.

Down by the riverside, brings our foothills well down into the central transition climate, with its short cold winters and long warm summers during which most of the rain falls. The

Fig 10 *How to read a climate diagram*

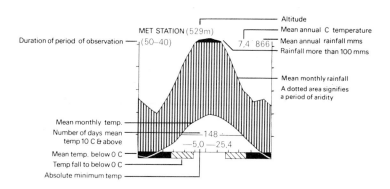

These are the keys to information contained in climate diagrams.

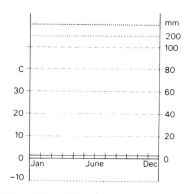

climate of Bavaria is ideal both for vegetation and for man, the warm rainy summers make for lush forests and rich crops, the snow of winter providing a protective blanket and winter sports.

Like most people, I like a warm dry holiday and therefore make no apologies for the fact that no less than four of the programmes bask in the climate of the Mediterranean.

The rain in Spain provides the full spectrum, from the driest to the wettest, castanets and all! While **The hanging gardens of Atlantis** take us down into the deep south with some alpine shocks up on the high mountains of Crete.

All from one small corner dwells both gastronomically and haute couturally on what man can do within the confines of an almost perfect climate; while **Doge City** shows what nature can do in a stucco jungle.

The way back north takes us into **No-man's-land** along the borders of Poland and Russia. It also takes us across the border between the predominantly deciduous woodland of the south-

Fig 11 *'Weather' I go in Europe (Opposite page)*

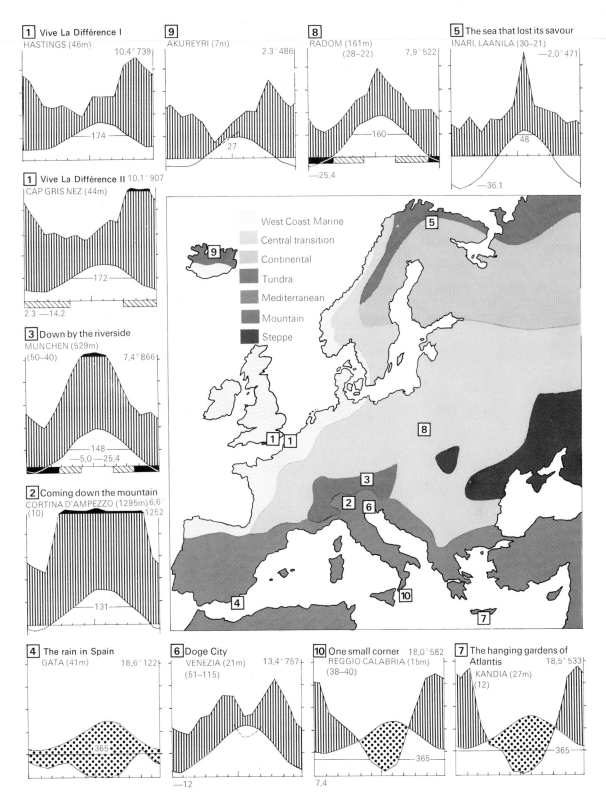

1 Vive La Différence I
HASTINGS (46m)
10,4° 739
—174—

9 AKUREYRI (7m)
2,3° 486
27

8 RADOM (161m)
(28–22)
7,9° 522
—160—
—25,4

5 The sea that lost its savour
INARI, LAANILA (30–21)
—2,0° 471
48
—36.1

1 Vive La Différence II 10,1° 907
CAP GRIS NEZ (44m)
—172—
2,3 —14,2

3 Down by the riverside
MUNCHEN (529m)
(50–40)
7,4° 866
—148—
—5,0 —25,4

2 Coming down the mountain
CORTINA D'AMPEZZO (1295m) 6,6°
(10) 1252
—131—

West Coast Marine
Central transition
Continental
Tundra
Mediterranean
Mountain
Steppe

4 The rain in Spain
GATA (41m)
18,6° 122
365

6 Doge City
VENEZIA (21m)
(51–115)
13,4° 757
—12

10 One small corner 18,0° 582
REGGIO CALABRIA (15m)
(38–40)
365
7,4

7 The hanging gardens of Atlantis
KANDIA (27m)
(12)
18,5° 533
365

23

ern part of the mixed forest zone, towards the coniferous forests of the Boreal.

My farthest north was Lake Inari where Finland, Norway and Russia meet and the tundra has its beginnings, north of the **Sea which lost its savour.** Iceland, though farther south, lies all by itself as if hanging from the Arctic Circle. Its southwest coasts bathe in the warmth of the North Atlantic Drift and its northern shores are frozen by the pack-ice of the East Greenland Current. In consequence, the southern part of Saga Land was probably clothed in open birch forest, its bulk, as most of it is today, dominated by the stunted communities so typical of the Tundra. This is the land of hot springs and volcanoes, the land where **Some like it hot.**

Iceland is, in fact, that depression to which our weather men (sorry, weather persons) refer. It is the place in which the weather patterns of the oceanic fringe of Europe are generated.

All that leaves just one major climatic/vegetational belt unaccounted for, and that is the Steppes. All I can do is apologise for the omission and say that, perhaps, we will get there next time.

Hang about! There is just one more map. Looking out of the windows of whatever it is you travel in, you are likely to see an awful lot of agricultural land. The last map shows the limits of the major crops and hence the way in which man is limited by the potential of the environments of Europe. It just might help you to locate yourself, that is if you have forgotten your flora.

Fig 12 *The northern limits of some important members of the EEC. Economic plants of course*

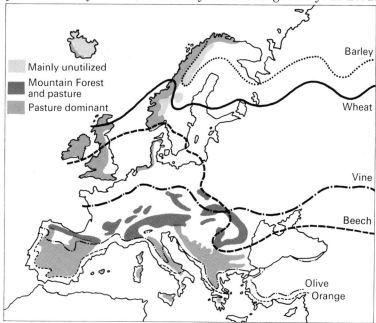

Mainly unutilized

Mountain Forest and pasture

Pasture dominant

Barley

Wheat

Vine

Beech

Olive
Orange

Coming down the mountains

An 'Alp' is, by definition, an area of upland pasture to which cows are taken to graze, but only in the summer. You know, Alps are the light green bits amongst the dark green forest, high up on the picture post-card mountains.

'The Alps' is the collective name for a whole group of mountain ranges which support the majority of the alps – and much of the picture post-card industry of Europe.

Alpine is the name given to the climate which predominates at altitudes above about 1,000 metres, at least in central Europe, and to the flora which typifies these mountain environs, including many of those which feed the lucky cows that help to produce that wonderful milk chocolate!

The Alps proper have their roots at the coast near Monaco and include in their sweeping compass the Maritime, Savoy, Cottian, Pennine (that makes you feel at home!), Bernese, Otzal, Bergamo, Chaetian, Bavarian, Carnic, Venetian and Julian, to name but a few; ending back at the sea with the Dinaric Alps close to Split in Yugoslavia. Each one could be regarded as a range or massif in its own right, but together they make up the Alps which spreads a lot of 'alpineness' over an arc of more than 1,000 kilometres.

This is the area of Europe most guaranteed to make the average British botanist go a little ga-ga and the average British horticulturalist get a severe twitch of the sponge-bag fingers. The symptoms of the former are a look of blank astonishment and a very tattered copy of 'Polunin's Mountain Flowers'. Those of the latter are much worse, the temptation being to dig up the choice plants, secreting them among soaps and after-shave, where the majority will die long before they get back home. Three words of warning – 'Don't do it'. For a start, there are laws banning the importing of live plant material into Britain without a licence and, for a finish, we would be the first to grumble if them foreigners came over here and pinched our plants.

I know the temptation all too well. All I have to do is set foot off a cable car and I get a touch of the 'Julie Andrews', leaping about in slow motion, my fingers just itching to pick a bunch of flowers. I argue with myself that it doesn't really matter because they will all be eaten or mowed down with the hay. However, a

Fig 13 *Round leaved Wintergreen Pyrola rotundifloria*

Fig 14 *Serrated leaved Wintergreen Orthilia secunda*

Fig 15 *King Olaf's Candlestick Moneses uniflora*

look back down the track at all the other tourists always stops me in mid pick. The fact is that, today, there are just too many tourists and each one tends to be very selective, picking only the choicest blooms. So much so that, in places, the alpine flora is in real danger and, once it has gone it is very difficult, if not impossible, to replace.

Having got all that off my chest, at least temporarily, I feel the time has come to wend my way round the mountain and, in the absence of pink pyjamas, I have chosen a range of pink mountains, the Dolomites.

South over the Brenner Pass and turn left or, if your car will stand it, how about north, south, east and west up and down the hairpins of the Gros Glockner and then turn right. There to the south of the road, in the high middle distance you will see some peaks unlike any you have yet passed, knife edges of pink rock, each with an icing of fresh snow. Once you have passed the sign which reads 'Cortina d'Ampezzo 29 km' you are right in among them – the Dolomites proper or, to bring them into EEC line, the Dolomitic Alps.

The road climbs up through the dark spruce forests, with long shots of higher and higher peaks, it runs beside clear green-blue lakes, through gorges where mountains sprout straight out of the tarmacadam and, eventually, it drops spectacularly down into the valley of Cortina.

I have driven that road on no less than twenty-two occasions and I still get just as excited. Without doubt, the best thing to do is to arrive in Cortina just as dawn begins to light up the peaks. It is only during the period between first light and the moment the sun appears over the top of the Crystal Mountain, shafting warmth into the valley, that the peaks seem to have any bulk at all. Once the sun is out in full, they appear as if mere cardboard cut-outs, backdropped to set off the beauty of the valley.

It is in this misty foredawn that it is best to take to the forests, for then the shy Hazel Hen may be caught off guard as fawns play in the mists of the forest paths. This is the time to see the full cross section of the family of wintergreens, the *Pyrolaceae*, a family which is closely related to that of the heathers and heaths. The wintergreens are all herbs and, what is more, they are all partial saprophytes, living always in close association with the raw humus of the forest floor. *Pyrola* itself has a tall spike around which the waxlike flowers are arranged in perfect array. *Orthilia*, the serrated wintergreen, has its flowers set secund, that is all nodding to one side. While *Moneses uniflora* (perfection personified in the name of King Olaf's Candlestick) has a single wax-white flower, the ovary and style providing the stem of the candlestick and the anthers the decoration around its base. But I am jumping the gun – this chapter was meant to start at the top!

When in Cortina, the only trouble is to know at which top to start, there are so many of them. So I do as the Cortinarians do, go to the Embassy Coffee House to sit and think about which peak to take in and, while so doing to take in a few cream cakes, and what cream cakes!

When we were making the programme which goes with this chapter, I was determined to show the affluent grandeur of this place, where the environment offers almost boundless potential to both man and nature. Well, I reckoned that the Embassy Coffee House summed it all up and so we went along to the tourist office and asked, 'would it be possible to film in and around the Embassy?' Answer, 'yes', and 'would it be possible to have a Lamborghini parked outside?' Answer 'what colour?' We chose yellow; but, sorry, I am again jumping the story: Back to the peaks and today it's Mount Tofane.

Three magnificent cable cars take you up, up, up and, so as not to spoil the botanical sights of the descent, it is best to keep your eyes on the view. Looking back, you get the feeling of going through a giant zoom lens in reverse, the vista becoming more expansive in scope, though less clear in detail. Cortina is a picture postcard town, neat houses, cuckoo clock around the nursery slopes which, if you are there at the right time, and the right time is spring or autumn, are a blue haze of crocusses. There are two sorts of crocusses, belonging to two different natural orders. Look down the top of the flower and count; if there are three anthers it is a member of the *Iridaceae* and its name will be *Crocus*. In contrast, if there are six anthers it is a member of the lily family, *Liliaceae* and its name will be *Colchicum*. There are several different species of crocus, some flowering in spring and others in autumn, but all the *Colchicums* are autumn flowering. The autumn *Colchicum* is an amazing plant for, apart from producing its almost too-perfect flower, it also lives up to both its names, flowering in autumn and producing colchicine, a chemical which has some startling properties. All plants start life as a single cell which contains all the information needed for a productive life. As the plant grows so the cells divide, and the living information which is contained in information banks called chromosomes has to be duplicated. Colchicine mucks it all up allowing the process to get no further than duplicating the chromosomes. The result is a cell which is stuffed so full of information that there is little room for anything else and the cell may therefore die. The really fascinating question is the mechanism by which the

Fig 16 *Lathyrus luteus plus insect visitor*

autumn crocus produces colchicine in large amounts and yet continues to get its own cell divisions right every time! Whatever the answer, the abundance of colchicum blue on the nursery slopes is proof enough that *Colchicum autumnale* has learned how to live with its problem.

There is another important distinction between the autumn and spring flowering crocusses. Those which perform in the autumn produce a single flower which pokes up above the ground all by itself with no leaves at all. It is only in the following spring that the leaves appear, to feed the developing seed pod and replenish the underground stores ready for next autumn's flower.

Looking forward and upwards from the cable car the view is somewhat truncated by one of the largest sticks of pink rock in Europe and, although it doesn't say 'Cortina', it certainly does say 'Dolomite' all the way through. The bluish-pink limestone was laid down during the mesozoic period around 200 million years ago. Apart from the fact that Dolomitic limestone is full of its own character it is also full of fossils – sea urchins, crinoids, ammonites and a whole variety of shells. They are well worth keeping a look out for on the way down and, if you are not lucky enough to find some of your own, you can at least ogle at them in the shops back down in the town. If you can read Italian, there is a smashing book called 'Geologia fossili attorno a Cortina d'ampezzo' and it is sold at Foto Ghedina and in the bookshops and, if your Italian is a bit rusty, the photographs are in English! The author is one of the most fascinating people I have ever met and his name is Rinaldo Zardini. Professore Zardini is the local natural historian and, what he doesn't know about the plants, animals and fossils of the area probably isn't really worth knowing.

Once at the top of the last span of the cable car, the real alpine environment suddenly hits you. The sun may well be blazing down but, nevertheless, there is always a distinct nip in the air, and that's what alpine environment is all about! It's goose-pimple cold, way up there and, for much of the year, much of the summit is covered with a blanket of wonderful 'get your skis on type' snow, and around the summit of Mount Tofane, some of it will last the whole year round.

Europe in the round, all 360 degrees of it, awaits your all seeing pleasure after a short scramble to the tourists' lookout, the real summit being a not too easy walk away. However, even from this first point of vantage, you can see the mountains stretching away in cloud clad glory, row upon row of them.

Now, the descent of a lifetime is about to begin. If you are a first-class skier well, in season you can do it all the way, or a

Fig 17 *Some Fossils from the Rocks around Cortina (Collected and prepared by Rinaldo Zardini, Cortina D'Ampezzo)*
Numbers:
1-16 *Echinoderms*
1, 2, 3, 4, 5, 6, 7, 8, 13 and 15 *spines from Sea Urchins*
9, 10, 11, 12 *parts of the tests (bodies of sea urchins)*
15 *Part of a Sea Lily*
16 *Section of the 'Stem' of a Sea Lily*
17-20 *Brachiopods, Lamp Shells*
21-32 *Molluscs (Snails) with one shell*
33-37 *Molluscs with two shells*
38-42 *Ammonites, the shells of octopus-like animals*

first-class climber could make the total descent. If you have neither of these attributes, then take the cable car down the first two stages, but pause at each level to take 'alpenstock' of the delights of European high life at its best, starting at the edge of the Biosphere.

The Biosphere is the envelope of life which evolution has thrown around this fabulous planet of ours. Passing from the North Pole to the Equator the biosphere is zoned, ice desert, tundra, taiga, etc, etc, each zone exhibiting the potential of the environment. In like manner the Biosphere is zoned in vertical array wherever altitude provides a vertical series of contrasting environments.

Fig 18 Going up!
The vegetation changes

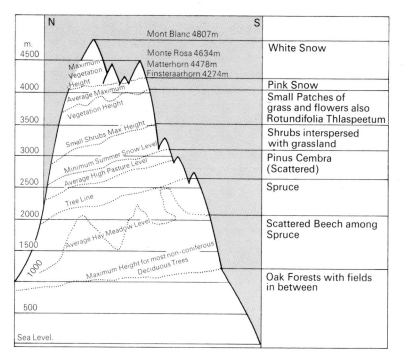

The permanent snow and ice of the top of Tofane, which stands a mere 3,243 metres, dwarfed by the 4,807 metres of its largest European brother is, at least for the present, beyond evolution for the simple, or rather very complex, reason that life has not yet overcome the problem of making use of solid water. Yet, even here in this white desert there is one plant that has learned the secret of living amidst the crystals of summer snow-melt. Its name is *Chlamydomonas nivea* and it turns the surface layers of snow an indelicate pink-red as its cells multiply in the long days of its short alpine summer which may last only a few weeks.

Red snow is a common feature of the peaks around Cortina and it is a fitting prelude to the life which unfolds down on the lower slopes; perfect in every way, evolution has adapted the Snow Alga to its own mode of productive life up in the cold.

Stepping down across the edge of the Biosphere is one of the most fascinating experiences of all, for this is the real edge of evolution. As the summer draws back the mantle of snow, it reveals dark, water soaked humus studded with plants whose leaves are blanched white, etiolated by growing in the darkness beneath the snow. The same thing happens to the grass if you leave the dustbin lid or some other opaque object on the lawn.

Etiolated they may be, but some of the plants will already be in flower and, if you are very careful, it is possible to locate a flower under the snow and excavate its delicate perfection.

Two of the most abundant beneath-the-snow flowers are *Soldanella alpina* and *Soldanella minima*, both members of the primrose family, together they typify the late snow patches.

Flowering is an active process and, like all other life processes, it produces heat as a waste product and that heat can help to melt the snow. Add to this the fact that both the flower bud and flower stalk are dark, almost black-green, and black absorbs heat and you have it, Soldenella's secret snow-melting formula! Each plant melts its own personal ice cave in which the flower head develops safe from all the cold snaps of a late spring.

At first sight the Soldanellas may not appear to have much in common with the true primroses, only close inspection reveals the features which prove the family ties. Almost as if to help you in your genealogical determinations, there are plenty of real primroses to be found in the environs of the snow banks, including the diminutive *Primula minima* and the much more splendid *Primula splendens*. They are real primrose-looking primroses, the only thing which spoils the illusion is that they are pink. The fact is that only one of the high alpine primroses and that is the Bear's Ear, *Primula auricula*, is yellow and is a plant of the rock crevices, not of the high alpine meadows. Almost as if to confuse the poor British botanist, it grows alongside the Pink Tormentil, *Potentilla nitida*, which just goes to prove that it isn't the colour that really matters.

King amongst the plants of the rocky outcrops and especially the eroded gravels is the Alpine Penny Cress, *Thlaspi rotundi-folia*, its neat cushions of round fleshy leaves being so typical of the cushion-like growth habit of the majority of the plants which thrive in this harsh habitat. On the more vertical slopes no protective snow cover will remain and so the plants appear to draw comfort from their own cushion-like form.

It may seem bad enough that we botanists name all our plants in Latin, but I will let you into a secret, some of us also give Latin names to the plant communities and this, one of the highest of all is called the *Thlaspeetum rotundifoliae*, don't worry, I can't say it either!

From here on down it's 'Sound of Music' scenery all the way and the thing that sets the botanists feet all of a twitter is the fact that you can't put 'em down without treading on some prize specimen. So instead of just producing a long list of adulatory Latin, allow me to burst into verse.

A's for *Azalea*, mountain of course
And B is for *Bartsia* which grows in the north.
C for *Campanula* that grow here in droves,
While *Daphne striatum* smells not unlike cloves.
E is for Eidelweiss, leave it, don't pick,
The laws of the country say a fine or the nick!
G is for Gentian, what else could it be?
Horminium pyreniacum is easy to see.
Iberis sempervirens comes next on my list,
For *Juniperus nana* is so easy to miss.
Kobresia is tall and looks just like a sedge,
And alpine lilies gild many a ledge.
Moneses uniflora, Wintergreen (see above),
Nigretella nigra, Black Orchid I love.
Oreochloa distica is the grass of the heights,
Alpine poppies are yellow, some buttercups white!
Quercus is the Oak, there's one down below,
Rhodothamnus chamaecystus, Alpine Rose don't you know.
From the *Saxifragaceae* there are many to choose,
Thalitricum alpinum is one of the Rues.
U is for umbel, a cartwheel of flowers
And Varrow's in here 'cos it stuck me for hours
Veronica, Verbascum, Veratrum and all
Alpine Violets are yellow and the Pine trees so small.
Now Wormwood's a name that might make you chuckle
While *xylosteum* is specific for a Honeysuckle.
Oh Z, what a problem, I was going to ignore 'er,
But *Bromus* is *Zerna* in the up-to-date flora.

Sorry about that, but it might just help you to get your tongue round some of the Latin names, or even rush off and buy one of the many super illustrated floras so that you can see what I am rhyming about. If you do the latter and there are a lot to choose from, may I suggest that you invest in one that

Opposite Page
Alpine Bouquet, Cortina Style

Top left
Alpine Poppy

Top right
Globe Flower

Middle left
Trumpet Gentian

Middle right
Spring Gentian

Bottom left
Soldanella

Bottom right
Round Leaved Thlaspi

fits in your pocket. I am on my third and it is already falling to pieces, well loved, well used and well soaked in melted ice.

The air is getting warmer and usually by this stage in the descent, I have finished my sandwiches and commended the crumbs to the alpine ants. Looking down, there are fingers, no wedges of dark green extending up the slope, rather like the teeth of some gigantic shark which is engulfing the mountain. Almost without noticing it, I have been walking all morning in the topmost branches of the high alpine mini-forest, whose mighty willows, *Salix arbuscula, herbacea, reticulata* and all,

Fig 19 *A mature willow tree trunk catkins and all, forty-two years old and only 5 cm tall*

raise slender trunks up to the amazing height of around 5 cm. Now you are edging towards the real forest fringe, a forest of *Pinus montana* which, although never reaching any great height, grows in such masses that together they form an effective break to all but the largest avalanches. The normal snowfall is also intercepted by the mass of branches and forms a white, fluffy umbrella, beneath which life can go on, protected from the worst effects of the winter wind.

It is within this shelter that the Chamois Deer find some protection at the onset of winter and, even in summer, if you sit

Opposite Page

Top
The Pupplinger Au, Dynamic Diversity (Chapter Three)

Bottom
The Cloisters of the Carmina Beurana (Chapter Three)

quietly within the forest fringe, you may be rewarded with a close up view of these not so tiny creatures. They often go bounding about on the screes which separate the fingers of the forest – just like they do on the adverts! They are, however, not advertising whatever it is, but are shamming the display of the rutting season. One of my prided possessions is a single tiny antler with its typical downward twist, which I was lucky to find on one of my descents down to Cortina. The shy Chamois, like all members of the deer family, shed and grow a new set each year.

Scattered among the twisted Mountain Pines are a few more stately trees, so stately that they look out of place amongst all the other stunted vegetation. If you are in search of rare plants, it is usual to keep your eyes down at ground level and look for something rather small and insignificant. The stately *Pinus cembra* is one of the rare plants that you really have to look up to for, although it's not rare at the right level in the right part of the Alps, it is only found in a narrow zone between the alpine forest proper and the open slopes above. This is the first plant that is 'stupid', or is it 'brave' enough to raise its branches and its leaves up above any hope of a protective snow blanket; and that is real bad news, especially in the annals of plant physiology. During the winter the ground may be frozen solid, shutting off the water supply to everything. Beneath a blanket of snow life isn't too bad because leaves and buds will not be exposed to desiccation by the wind. Water loss with no possibility of replacement could soon spell death for any plant which lacks the full gamut of adaptations. Add to this the fact that those winds can bring the temperature way down below freezing point and the problems of life above the snow become worse and worse.

Fig 20 *Pinus cembra...*

Fig 21 *...and its bunch of fives*

Pinus cembra, like all pines, has needle shaped leaves but, unlike our home-growing Scots Pine, which has its needles in pairs, the Arolla Pine bears its needles in bundles of five. All the young needles fit tightly together, their faces, from which most of the water loss would take place, are turned inwards and are thus effectively shut off from the outside world. In winter I have seen the leaves tightly clamped together in a sheath of ice which must provide added protection from water loss.

The proof of their physiology is in the growing and, as they grow there seemingly out of preference, the Arolla Pine must have overcome most of the problems of life at the forest limits. In recent years many plant physiologists have set to work to study these stalwart plants – and who can blame them, there can be no better place in which to do field work, winter or summer. Much of the work has been done on the much commoner and more economically important Spruce, *Picea abies*, which, although finding its main habitat lower down the mountain slopes, does grow in very exposed situations.

It is now known that, as winter approaches, these hardy plants begin to prepare for the cold to come by a process known as 'frost hardening'. In some ways it is rather akin to filling with anti-freeze! Lots of sugar is stored in the leaf sap, lowering its freezing point and, at the same time the living cytoplasm undergoes a series of, what are as yet poorly understood, changes which make it even more unlikely that the actual living tissues will freeze. It now seems clear that it is not the low temperatures themselves which cause the damage but the formation of ice crystals within the living cells. Water expands as it freezes and, just like your water pipes, the cells will become deformed and the living process will break down.

In the non hardened condition of early autumn Spruce, needles can be killed at a temperature of only $-7°C$, whereas when in winter condition they can live through temperatures of $-40°C$ or even $-60°C$.

The really interesting point is that a greater resistance is developed in a cold winter than in a mild one. Real damage is only caused by an early frost before the Spruce is hardened or a late one after dehardening has taken place. Once the latter process has occurred it is all systems grow for a productive spring; new wood to lift all those new needles up towards the sun.

So it is that the vegetation gets taller and taller as you get lower down the mountain. Red snow to *Thlaspeetum*, to alps, to Mountain Pine, Arrola Pine, next deciduous Larch, its branches in the damp air hung with lengths of Spanish Moss which is, in actual fact, a lichen; and then you are down within the skirt of the spruce forest which at one time went clear on to Cortina itself. These zones are of course not clear cut; the exact altitude at which one ends and the next one starts will depend on the angle of slope of the mountain and whether it is facing north, south, east or west. This is why I have not quoted a series of altitudes relating to my descent. The other reason is that man has, for a long time, been working on the mountain slopes. In the past many of the lower slopes have been cleared and now form extensions of the alps, linking them up with the meadows of the valley bottom. The function of these open swathes was to feed the herds of cows in the spring and produce enough hay for winter feeding. They are man created and man maintained and, if you were under the impression that we humans 'never did no good nowhere' in the countryside, then go to Cortina or, come to that, to any of the Alps and take a good look!

This is the place in which to learn your plants, 200 plus is an easy total to tot up as you wend your way down. Even if you are not that energetic you can see most of them from a car, as there is a good motor road to almost within reach of the tree line.

Like all natural patterns, the one around Cortina is changing; the skiers are demanding new runs and new swathes are being cut through all the alpine forest zones, the resultant slopes are being thatched with straw and diesel oil, then grass is sown to complete the job. Not even the high slopes nor the peaks are safe. The whirr of the wings of flocks of Alpine Choughs are now drowned by the harsh roar of the alpine bulldozer as the mountains are given, not only new ski-lifts, but also new face lifts to extend the delights of the piste. Ominous as all this may seem, perhaps the worst innovation is the introduction of sheep instead of cows on the high grazings and of motor scythes instead of hand sickles on the lower slopes. It's quicker? Yes. It's cheaper? Yes, but perhaps the full diversity of the alpines cannot adapt to the pressure of these new regimes of 'grazing'.

Please, this is a place where we must get it all right and, sitting back in the Embassy, my pocket flora just a little bit more tatty, I get the feeling that perhaps they are beginning to get the formula worked out. Just enough development to open up just enough of the mountains so that everyone can take their own form of alpine enjoyment. Skiing and all that goes both before and 'apres', winter holidays and a summer overflowing with flowers, potential for everyone and cream cakes in the Embassy – what more could anyone want?

Down by the riverside

There are many ways of coming down a mountain, some are fast and painful, the majority more staid and enjoyable. Whichever happens to be your favourite method of descent mine, at least when leaving the Alps, is to follow the river Isar, as it flows down through the affluence of Bavaria to and through the great city of Munich.

It is the original 'wunderbar' sort of river, which rises in the heights of the massif that culminates in the peaks of the Zugspitze, Germany's highest mountain, and sparkles its way down over a series of dizzy waterfalls. Wherever the rain collects to feed the headwaters, the limestone rocks are blackened by growths of blue-green algae, which deepen the shadows, giving the effect of an over zealous lighting man at a massive son et lumière. This is a fitting backdrop to the Bavarian countryside.

Bavaria is the land of songs which tell of a good life, a life of plenty with food and beer flowing free, of après ski in the winter and lakes crowded with the sunworshippers of summer who are all at 'See'. Perhaps the most famous of the Bavarian songs are the Carmina Burana, discovered in the Baroque monastery at Benediktbeuern. Songs that were written, not to commemorate the founding of this work of religious architecture, but in adulation of the affluence of a countryside and a way of life that allowed, not only the saturation of the desires of the flesh, but the construction of, what is to me, the best of all Baroque.

But why all this affluence? 1,400 mm of rain each year, much of it falling in the long, warm summer. Rich soils made from a mixture of rocks ground down from the diversity of the alps by the ice sheets of the past. Cold winters with frosts enough to cleanse and stir the soil and yet with a blanket of snow to protect the dormant shoots. Add to this almost perfect mélange of environment, the valleys brim full of lakes each brim full of fish and a complex of forests, with venison on the hoof and you have the answer. A landscape with enough potential to satisfy both man and nature.

The twin towers of Kloster each capped with a copper green onion, dominate the landscape, dwarfing the famous youth hostel and the houses which, with true teutonic precision, parade the streets. Standing back, out of the main order, set amongst the cool shade of trees, is the headquarters of the local foresters, demonstrating in its quiet almost forgotten old world affluence, the main link between man and the real productivity of natural Bavaria.

For centuries the Bavarian forests have been managed for the production of 'Timber', but have, in the main, been managed with such skill that much of the diversity of forest life still remains. Mixtures of Spruce and Beech are found on the lower slopes, their straight trunks pushing upwards to hold the canopy of two contrasting greens aloft, where it intercepts the energy of the sun, channelling some of it into the production of wood. In like manner strong woody roots reach down and out, to borrow some of the materials needed for good growth temporarily from the rich soil. Each year the silent fall of leaves carry some of the nutrients back to the surface of the soil, where they swell the pool of available minerals. These, in turn, may pass to the diversity of herbs, each of which finds its own special niche in the cool shade of the structured forest.

The structure goes clear through from the highest leaves of the canopy, whose intricate arrangements may help to maximise interception of the light, down through the layers of the forest community. Saplings and mature shrubs produce the understorey, further enhancing the depth and patterns of shade. Lower still, ferns, herbs and seedlings, in their turn, shelter deep wefts of moss and leafy liverwort, always damp and cool. Below ground the structure is not lost, the shallow rooted plants at least isolate their demands for water and nutrients to the surface layers. As a rule of thumb it may be said that the plants which reach up the highest also send their roots down the deepest, not only in search of water and minerals, but in order to gain support for their woody weight.

One plant which appears to make the most of both the above and below ground worlds is the Asarabacca, *Asarum europaeum*. It is a perennial herb with a thick creeping underground stem that sends bunches of kidney shaped leaves up on long thin stalks. Each one has a dark green shiny surface (cuticle) which reflects all the sun flecks that pass across its shaded retreat. Apart from its name, the most surprising feature of the Asarabacca is its single flower, brown to lurid mauve in colour it grows out into the raw litter of leaves and twigs. If they do rise above the surface of the current years leaf fall, the flowers are probably pollinated by those busy flies which can make a rest in the forest such an annoying experience. They may, however, remain below the surface where there are many creepy crawlies to finish off the job and, if all

Fig 22 *Asarabacca*

else fails, self pollination ensures a plump capsule full of flat seeds and hence another generation. Working in the forest is always full of surprises, the interplay of light dappling down from above plays tricks, enhancing the complex patterns of the forest floor, making it difficult to recognise the plants from any distance. The surface carpet is dark green, jewelled with the pure white perfection of anemones and the nodding metallic blue drops which hang from the flowering scapes of the Wood Melick. *Aposeris foetida*, like a very neat and tidy dandelion, adds its own symmetrical variety, neat circles of accurately cut leaves from the centre of which rises a single slender flower stalk topped by a lemon yellow bloom. It also adds its own particular foetid smell to the sweet and rotten aroma of the forest, the smell emanating, not so much from the flower, but from its leaves crushed by passing feet.

It is possible to find areas of forest where, during the bad times of the past, the local peasants collected the annual fall of beech litter to use as bedding for their cattle. In these places, the natural cycle of nutrients has thus been broken, and the

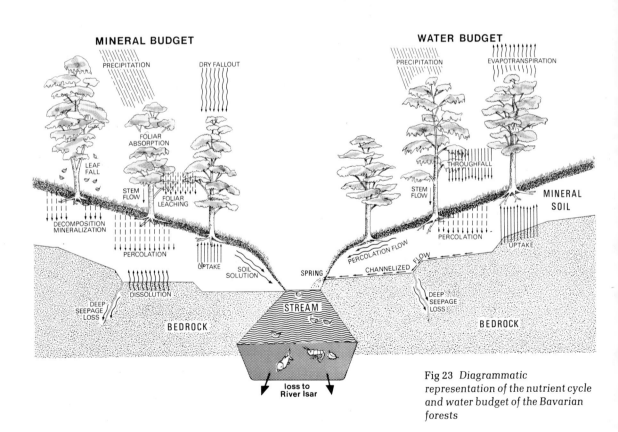

Fig 23 *Diagrammatic representation of the nutrient cycle and water budget of the Bavarian forests*

lush green carpet has been replaced by extensive stands of plants which demand less in the way of nutrients to satisfy their own particular way of life. Plants like the Bilberry and Bank Hair Moss immixed with another moss that has been aptly named the Vegetable Sheep, *Leucobryum glaucum*. Its resemblance to a sheep comes from the blanched, white-green foliage and the fact that it can grow into large rounded masses about the size and shape of a sleeping animal.

Of all the plants growing in this man-modified community, *Leucobryum* demonstrates its true individuality. It can assert its independence from the forest by detaching from the rich humus and gradually growing into a ball, a microcosm which may be rolled around the forest by passing animals. The ball rolling mode of life is termed aegrophilly and, although in the case of *Leucobryum*, it doesn't do much for the saying 'a rolling stone gathers no moss', it does demonstrate the break up of the society of the forest floor. A careful study of the distribution of this moss will, however, show that, although it appears to be a lone operator, it still is absolutely dependent on the nutrients which are washed off by the rain from the canopy high above. The main and most luxuriant vegetable sheep, whether attached or not, are usually found 'sleeping' around the bases of trees where stem flow, that is the rain draining down the tree trunks, enriches the soil.

Please, if you are lucky enough to find one of these singular plants, roll it about by all means, but leave it in the forest positioned ready for the next shower of nutrient enriched rain. Likewise, be very careful when reading the forest signs. Not all the areas of Bavarian forest which are carpeted with Bilberry and the promise of rolling mosses have been produced by litter pickers of the past. Many such areas are of perfectly natural occurrence, being in forests developed on acid soils, the natural structure of the forest reflecting the potential of the site.

The secret of good management is to keep the cycle of death and re-growth turning, thereby maintaining the flow of minerals from the soil to the leaves and back to the soil again. If this can be done, then the only losses which must be made good are the nutrients that are carried away out of the system in the cut timber.

Under completely natural conditions the losses from the closed cycle of forest life are very small. Animals may feed in the forest moving out into the wet meadows beside the river, but it is a two way traffic and in fact there is much evidence to show that the bulk of the movement is the other way. The animals who live in the forest will move out into the grass-lands to feed, returning with a new load of nutrients which are deposited in the privies of the woodland. The only real losses from the system are twigs, leaves and other small bodies which, falling into the streams and rivulets which water and drain the forest are carried away out of the system.

The same is true for the fruits and seeds. The majority of them are eaten by ravening hoards of birds, mammals and insects which depend on these fruits of the forest for their particular livelihood. A few of the propagules escape to maintain the population of seedlings and saplings and hence the future structure of the forest. Only those which fall into flowing water may be lost from the system altogether, and the destiny of these natural exports will be the fast turbulence of the river Isar, where they will rub seedcoats with similar exports from the high life way up near the top of the Alps.

Trunks, branches, twigs, leaves, flowers, fruits, seeds, yes even vegetable and real sheep that fall into the drainage system may be carried along downstream. Their travels will only be terminated when some eddy, reverse current or bend in the river provides shelter enough for the flowing water to shed its organic load.

24 km south of Benediktbeuern, and that is measured as the hooded crow flies, not as the Isar flows, the waters of this young river meet and mingle with those of a lesser stream, the Loisach, from whence their swollen mass flows on towards and beyond Munich.

Their confluence is, to say the least, a place of great turbulence, a glorious mixture of milk-green water and bare white shingle, the former always breathtakingly cold, the latter heated almost to frying point by the sun. In the summer it is a playground for the less inhibited of vital statistics from München und Umgebung. Amongst the wedges of cool green willow and pine forest, the lederhosen and dirndl are laid aside and obesity is mellowed in the sizzle of Ambre Solaire. When the heat is too much to bare, there is always the Isar, still ice cold for, only a few hours ago it was ice, melting on the high peaks, waiting to whisk you away, off down river! At first, the rate is alarming, being measured in bumps rather than knots, but soon you learn the ways of the water and come to accept it as the way to travel. The only problem is to steer clear of the shallow bits and to regain the bank without losing several centimetres of skin, or worse.

After a hard day's botanising in the forests around Wolfratshausen there is nothing better than a quick float down the river, especially when you remember that there are all those extra forest exports floating along with you. There is an absolutely smashing bit where, if the flow is right, and you can

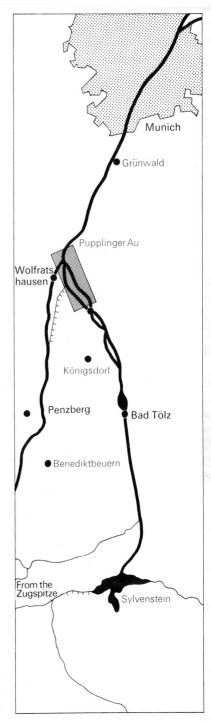

Fig 24 *Cold flows the Isar*

flowing water
vegetation of gravel and sand
heath and open
pine forest
willow scrub with
Tamarisk
broad leaf scrub
and forest

Fig 25 Map of the vegetation of the Pupplinger Au, a pattern of Dynamic diversity

keep in the main current, you actually get dragged under-water for a considerable distance before you are shot out onto a gravel bar. This is, of course, not the best form of travel for anyone other than an experienced swimmer, but there is no getting away from the fact that it is the most exhilarating of nature trails. The river takes you through a protected area, a statutory nature reserve called the Pupplinger Au, the wonders of which start right at the edge of the water.

Among the pebbles and larger rocks there is a scatter of plants, each rooted firmly into the silts that have collected between the stones. They are a motley array, gathered together from a variety of habitats, including the highest of the Alps: Spring and Trumpet Gentians, Chamois Cress, Gypsophila and Alpine Toadflax, all perfectly adapted to withstand the rigours of higher alpine life, find similar conditions in which they must flower and fruit while the growing is good, down by the river-side.

Even in the height of summer, a short sharp shower way back up the valley may turn the more placid Isar into a scream-ing torrent which, overflowing its summer banks, tears at any life exposed on the open single. Only those plants which have already fruited may survive the onslaught of the waters, for their next generation wiil sail away down towards Munich where, if they are lucky, they may grace the banks of the river in the capital of Bavaria. Each year the likelihood of their survival gets less and less for below Wolfratshausen much of the banks are man made, edged with ordered embankments that provide no safe rootholes and etched with summer-houses, the river has been tamed into, at least partial, sub-mission. Only in the more natural areas upstream does the perennial interplay of flood and stability keep the habitat open enough to allow these delicate plants to re-establish themselves anew each year.

So it is that the Müncheners are drawn to this amphitheatre of river gravel to savour the delights of an alpine garden, self sown and self perpetuating. Many glorious hectares in various stages of colonisation, from shingle banks, through the gentle swaying groups of willows that act as traps for other materials downwashing with the floods of spring, to the stable order of the climax forests.

Moving away from the roar of the river, the scene rapidly changes from the white glare of the washed gravel to the cool green of the willow scrub, interspersed with the prickly presence of stunted Juniper and small Pines, pioneering the forest that is following on behind. The open pine forest has an almost fairytale appearance and is packed full of botanical

Fig 26 Tamariskenfleur
(extreme left)

Fig 27 Spring Gentian

Fig 28 Chamois Cress
(extreme left)

Fig 29 Alpine Toadflax

Fig 30 Trumpet Gentian

surprises. Above the smell of crushed juniper the air is heavy with a scent which is very reminiscent of those carnation-tasting sweeties that have unfortunately disappeared from the confections of modern confectioners. The smell emanates from the crowded pink spikes of a massive form of the Fragrant Orchid, which may grow as much as a metre tall.

Fortunately, the area is a nature reserve and, although betretten is not verboten, removal of plants is. So it is possible in early summer to regale yourself with the sight of thousands of Europe's most flamboyant of orchids, the Lady's Slipper. I'm afraid that it would appear that even the locals can't understand the German notices for, sadly, many of the spikes are removed long before they have time to set seed.

One of the great curiosities of the Pupplinger Au is the Tamariskenfleur, *Tamarix gallica*, its grey-green foliage and long sprays of pink flowers looking out of place in the alpine foreland. It is in fact a plant of the Mediterranean, which finds its northern limit here in the heat thrown up from the washed river gravel. A close relative of the Tamariskenfleur is *Tamarix mannifera* which grows in the desert of Sinai, where it produces a sweet gummy exudate – the Manna of the Bible.

The walk up from the river is not a gradual one, the banks are terraced and the higher one goes up the terraces the more stable are the conditions and the denser and more mature the forest. There are, however, areas where the river, swollen by a period of extra rapid snow melt, has flowed through a section of mature forest, scouring out the gravel from the upstream side of each tree. In consequence, all the trees lean in a drunken manner, at the same angle and pointing in the same direction. Even more peculiar, the depressions caused by the scouring are often occupied by a single shrub, which seemes as out of place as would lederhosen on Clapham Common. The shrub in question is *Ligustrum officinale*, the ever so amenable to clipping front garden Privet. The natural habitat of the Privet is in damp woodland and, in its natural form its straggling branches bear white sprays of sweet smelling flowers, a sight rarely seen in its garden setting for, in our ardour for topiary, we often chop them off.

Beyond the drunken trees of the flood plain, the riverside forests gradually merge into the skyline grandeur that is Bavaria, a grandeur on which the wealth of the Bavarians was first founded.

It is true that man has, in the past, removed much of the forest from the flatter, most productive, land; replacing it with lush pasture and meadow, their productivity drawing upon the same nutrient store in the fertile 'forest' soils. In summer the cattle graze the sweet fields, producing milk in litres and beef and veal in surfeit. Each bale of hay reaped dry from the meadows is full of a great variety of seeds and fruits, products of the flowers which painted the fields of spring. The sweet smelling harvest is stored in the vastness of the barns which appear to prop up the gigantic Swiss Cottage type houses, each may house several generations of the farming family and the farmer's stock.

The nutrients thus removed from the fields, to feed the over-wintering stock, drain down as sewage into dark tanks set below the farmyard and the farm, from whence they will be returned to the fields when the growing time is right.

I once enjoyed life on one of these farms for a few glorious days, and one of my chores was to help lift the wooden cover from off the top of the cess pit and insert a great wooden pole to stir the thixotropic mass of nutrient into a ductile state. Once flowing, it was pumped into an elongated wooden cask on wheels and carted out into the fields where, trundling up and down it helped to complete the nutrient cycle. This is muck spreading, Bavarian style, but any old day just will not do for the conditions must be exactly right. If the sun is too hot, the strong liquid fertiliser will scorch the grass and the precious nutrients will be wasted. Likewise, if the day is too wet, all these hard won nutrients will wash straight off and into the Isar. So it must be just right.

The mechanisms of the modern farm have, at least in part, mucked it all up. The muck trucks are no longer shining examples of the cooper's craft, they are of sheet metal, zinc dipped and pulled by a purring tractor. Even the pumping is automatic and some have gone so far as taking the stuff direct to the fields through an automated network of pipes. The end-points are, however, the same, a smiling farmer waves the effluent in a friendly manner, a gay abandoned greeting, in the direction of all passing cars; an unmistakable aroma and fields full to overflowing with a new crop of grass.

Fig 31 *Guess who?*

So it is that the fields are full of more than promise as the magic process of recycling remains unbroken. Unfortunately, the innovations of modern Bavaria haven't stopped at the muck truck and its trappings. The delights of the land, its sun, rivers, lakes, forests and snowfields are no longer just the just reward for the hardworking farmers. The Carmina Beurana, schuplatter and the fame of the local festivals of light beer draw visitors to the promised land. The towns are overflowing with industry both light and not so light, the villages are either dormitories for Munich, or house the richest of summerhouses. The lakes overflow with camp sites where whole families take to the tent summer long, while father Volkswagens it back and forth to work.

All this is putting a new strain on the system and even the freshwaters of the Isar-Loisach confluence are no longer free from the taint of pollution. Now the Germans have rather a nice saying which, although it loses something both in translation and expurgation, reads something like this 'the Devil always relieves himself on the largest pile'.

Take a long slow walk back along the edge of the river as it roars its way through the Pupplinger Au. There amongst the frying heaps of flesh, the alpine plants are still all abloom in the clean gravel. Wherever a log or some other piece of flotsam has lodged on the banks, the scene is very different. In the lee of the object there is always a great accumulation of biological bric-a-brac, twigs, leaves, lumps of humus – the beginnings of a raw soil. The larger the object, the greater the pile and the more organic matter there will be present. More organic matter means fewer alpine plants, because their place is taken by ranker growing lowland weeds and even the seedlings of Willow, Pine and Spruce.

Downstream from any infall which carries sewage to the Isar the effect can be very marked. Even if no organic material escapes into the stream, the water itself will be enriched with nutrients and this will enrich the gravel banks, increasing their potential for the growth of everything. Add to this the fact that the friendly wave of the muck-spreading hose is being replaced, by the much more controllable whirr of machines dispensing pelletised fertilisers. No muck, no smell, no waste; well! Except for the fact that the natural stuff must go somewhere and, after treatment, the enriched waters flow into the Isar.

The Devil's pile gets larger and larger!

This, I am afraid, is not the end of my tale of woe. The other important feature of the Isar, at least so far as keeping the riverside in a more open, more juvenile state, are the flash floods of spring that tear away at the roots of the forest, opening up new patches, creating new ox-bows, new terraces, new land cleared for recolonisation. It was this ever shifting pattern of semi stability which characterised the confluence of the two rivers and gave it its unique character and vegetation.

The floods may well have been the creator and preserver of the Pupplinger Au, but they were also the destroyer and in-nundator of large parts of Munich, lower down stream. Already flood control measures are in massive operation. These include diversion of the rivers and the construction of an enormous dam with its impressive man-made lake, across which the road steps in boots of reinforced concrete. Already the reservoir has become a Mecca for watersporting types; and the head of much more permanent water provides power and coolant for new riverside factories on the banks of the Isar. All this is new affluence in this land which overflows with opportunities for man, if not today so much for nature.

Close beside the reservoir and overlooking the Seven League Bridge is a small automaton resplendent with four coloured buttons. It is capable, on payment, of reciting the tale of the building of the dam, a great feat of constructional engineering, extolling the benefits to mankind.

Although it can recite the tale in four languages, it doesn't even mention the Pupplinger Au, but why should it, probably no one ever told its programmer, and the same is probably true of the civil engineers who built the dam.

If they could stop the Isar apparently with such ease, surely they could find some way of building a little extra into their massive new system. Wouldn't it be possible, every now and again, to let the flood waters go, in a controlled way of course, so that they could do their scouring and cleaning act down by Wolfratshausen?

Is it too much to ask? I suppose all one can do is to hope that ways will be found to maintain the natural beauty of Bavaria to the full, and that the Pupplinger Au and its unique recycling system will not be allowed to pass into folk legend.

Rain in Spain

If you have one of those superior type atlases, the Cabo de Gata is probably marked in superior gothic type, if you haven't, well it's about halfway between Alicante on the ever so Costa Blanca and the peninsula of Gibraltar. Funny, I always thought it was an island.

An average year on the Cabo de Gata is enough to make a cactus feel thirsty, for 122 mm, which is only 12·2 cm to be exact, (and when you have got that little you have to be exact) of rain falls on every square metre of its sun baked surface. Standing on the coast and looking inland it is easy to see the cause of this aridity. Rising to a height of 3,482 metres is the main peak of the Sierra Nevada, a range of mountains which produces the most effective rain shadow in the whole of Europe. As the once water

Fig 32 *The rain in Southern Spain*

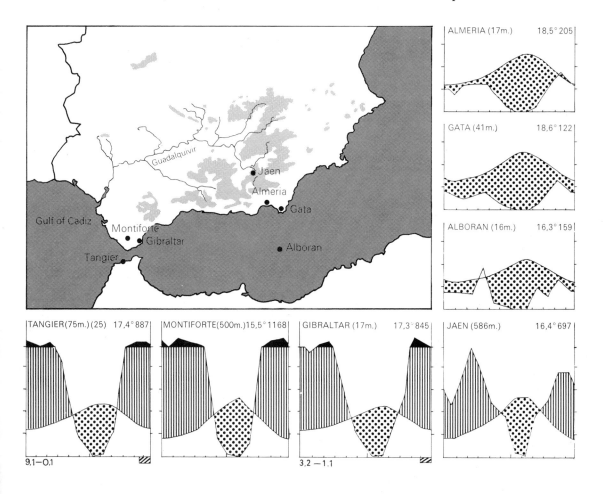

48

laden winds from the Atlantic rise up over this last barrier before the Mediterranean they lose their last drops of water with
the result that the average climatic data for the coastal strip
reads like the vital statistics of a Miss Death Valley competition.

It is no illusion, the bulk of the terrain supports only a very
sparse vegetation, consequently when the rains do come erosion
is the order of the storm stripping away any soil, exposing bare
rocks and producing a scene of water worn desolation.

What a place! I'm off, no need to take an umbrella or a flora,
nothing can grow in that, but as usual a flora goes into the case
for who knows, I just might get bored just bathing in the sun.

The fact is that no British-bred botanist should take on a holiday in Spain too lightly. Such a venture must be planned and
planned with great care if you are going to avoid the real shock
of being exposed to a real flora. Hold on to your passport, Spain
rejoices in having more than 6,000 different sorts of flowering
plants, just compare that with Britain's mere 1,700 or so, and
Spain shares with the Balkan peninsula the distinction of having Europe's most diverse flora.

Just why should it be that rich? For a start the Iberian peninsula has never suffered the recent depressions of a large ice cap
and thus it still retains many of its pre-ice-age plants. Next, is
the fact that the great continent of Africa isn't all that far away
as the migrating birds fly, and every year millions of them take
to the short sea route bringing with them all sorts of exotic
seeds. Then although the great lump of land is well connected
to the rest of Europe, the connection is blocked by the magnificent Pyrenees, a mountain barrier which sweeps from Irun on
the Bay of Biscay clear across to Port Bau on the Mediterranean.
So many of the members of the flora of the Spanish mainland

SOME EXAMPLES OF ENDENISM AMONGST SPANISH PLANTS

Latin Name of Genus	Common Name	Number of species in Spain	Approx. number of species endemic to Spain
Centaurea	Knapweed	90	50
Thymus	Thyme	31	24
Linaria	Toadflax	52	36
Genista	Greenweed	33	22
Cytisus	Broom	15	9
Ononis	Rest Harrow	41	17
Armeria	Thrift	30	23
Teucrium	Germander	35	20
Narcissus	Narcissus	45	20

Cork Oak
Quercus suber

have in glorious isolation gone their own way producing a good crop of endemics. Just compare.

Finally it must be realised that although the bulk of the package holidayers rush to the hot dry coastal strip, of all the countries in Europe, Spain has the greatest diversity of climates and the driest is that of the Cabo de Gata.

12·2 cm of rain is hardly enough to cover your ankles and is insufficient at that latitude to support anything except a semi-desert vegetation. The problems are however not just a dearth of water but also a superabundance of salt. When rain does fall it rapidly soaks into the dry soil dissolving minerals as it goes. As soon as the tap is turned off, evaporation becomes the main moving force and water rises again through the soil profile. At

Carob
Ceratonia siliqua

Sweet Chestnut
Castanea sativa

Holm Oak
Quercus ilex

Scots Pine
Pinus sylvestris

Allepo Pine
Pinus halepensis

Beech
Fagus sylvatica

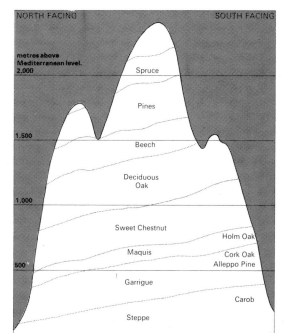

Silver Fir
Abies alba

Deciduous Oak
Quercus macrolepis

the surface, the water is lost but the minerals stay put and as the most abundant and soluble of all the minerals is plain salt, the soils therefore become saline adding to the problems of the plants already growing under the stress of too little water.

In consequence the vegetation from sea level to more than 700 metres in altitude is very reminiscent of that of the salt marshes which fringe the sea itself and many of the plants are salt loving or at least salt tolerant (halophytes). This type of vegetation is best called salt steppe and the reigning family of halophytes is the family of the goosefoots, or is it goosefeet, the *Chenopodiaceae* which get their name from their webbed leaves. The majority of the plants have fleshy leaves covered by thick waxy cuticles and an abundance of hairs and, at least for me, king of the saltys is *Mesembryanthemum crystallinum*. Although not a goosefoot it extols its latin name with leaves that are covered by a mass of transparent glossy vesicles which sparkle in the sun. It is in fact a member of another family the *Aizoaceae* which has made its own special habitat the more saline parts of the world.

The majority of the vegetation consists of a scatter of plants, well spaced out, their roots holding sway over a large area of soil, enough to provide their watery needs. There may however be another reason for this spacing out of the denizens of the semi-desert: many plants produce as waste products chemicals which can poison the soil making it less fit for the growth of other plants and even for their own seedlings. Under normal environmental conditions such chemicals would soon be washed away, but in a really dry environment they could accumulate and cause real problems. This pollute-it-yourself form of chemical warfare goes under the fancy name of allelopathy and it could be effective in keeping competitors at bay and account for some of the rather regular spacing of the plants of the Cabo de Gata.

Like all societies in which the growing is tough, come to think of it, like all societies plant or otherwise, there are always plenty of hangers-on. One plant overcomes the problems of life in a hot, dry, salty habitat and immediately others muscle in, reaping the benefits of their success. The vegetation of the salt steppe abounds with parasites, plants which, having no chlorophyll of their own parasitise the roots of others, pinching the nutrients of their unfortunate hosts, and some of these hangers-on are real weirdos. *Cynomonium coccinium* is one of the weirdest, seemingly so ashamed of its parasitic mode of life that the only part of the plant to rise above ground level is a fleshy, reddish black club shaped spike of flowers. *Cytinus hypocistis* though having the same dark side to its character, its flower is much

Fig 33 (opposite) *Not all the Mediterranean is hot and dry, go up any of its mountains and see how the vegetation responds to altitude*

Fig 34 *Cynomorium coccinium* (long shot)

Fig 35 *Cynomorium coccinium* (close-up) *showing anthers*

more beautiful looking not unlike a mass of yellow eggs set in a red basket. The latter is a member of a totally parasitic family which includes amongst its members the plant with the world's largest flower (measuring 1 metre across), *Rafflesia monstera*, a member of the flora of tropical forests. The parasites of Cabo da Gata may not be that big but some do keep very exclusive company as a number of their hosts are only found growing in that region, like the two saltworts *Salsola papillosa* and *Salsola genistoides*.

The illusion of a desert is confirmed by the presence of a number of plants which are in fact visitors from the deserts of the new world. The Prickly Pear, is a very prickly customer forming excellent hedges and an edible fruit, very tasty once you have removed the spines. *Agave*, the Century Plant, disobeys its name and flowers after about ten years of magnificent growth, the flower spike shooting up to an immense height of 10 metres in just a few weeks. It is almost as if this saps the strength of the plant which dies after flowering, its thick fleshy leaves collapsing to the ground. None of this particular plant monster is edible but the juice which flows from a cut flower spike when young may be fermented, the resultant beverage being Pulque, the national drink of Mexico.

A real desert succulent, and a real cactus; what more could one want from a desertscape? Answer, an oasis. Well you won't be disappointed for apart from the shimmering heat mirages that top every rise in the tarmacadam, there are real ones. Wherever the ground water comes to or near the surface, brown heat, becomes green coolth, complete with date palms and even paddy fields. No I am not suffering from drought stroke, they are as real as anything in the continent of Africa, genuine European wadis, and only a few miles as the pedalo pedals from the Costa de Package Holiday.

So if you want it dry you can't do any better than the Cabo da Gata, but you can get further south and to do that you must travel west to Tarifa. There Africa becomes an overpowering reality in the shape of Jebel Musa the Bald Mountain looming only 10 miles away from the other pillar of Hercules the Rock of Gibraltar, which together guard the mouth of the otherwise landlocked sea.

It was here that one of the first international protection rackets was evolved by the Moors, who took a toll from all passing ships – hence the word Tariff, although I don't think we got the word Mooring in the same way. The proof of the past presence of the Moors is in the architecture of this town and the proof that this is still an important trade route comes not only from the constant stream of boats which pass untariffed through the straits but the millions of birds which crowd the flightways of the spring and autumn migrations. Just how many pairs of eyes both human and avian have looked across the narrow strip of water in the knowledge of all the potential of another continent?

In 1928 one pair of eyes looked at the narrow neck of sea from an entirely different viewpoint. They belonged to Herman Sörgel, an engineer whose interest was in trying to bridge the gap with a dam, no, not to create a freshwater lake, exactly the opposite. His dream was to remove the Mediterranean, replacing it with fertile dry land, joining the two continents by evaporating the sea. Impossible? No! His calculations were quite correct, the sea could be removed. Every year the Mediterranean sun evaporates off 1,000 cubic miles of water, only part of this is replaced by inflow from the rivers. The deficit is made up by Atlantic water flowing in through the Straits of Gibraltar. Stop up the Straits and the Mediterranean would evaporate into thin air in a matter of 1,000 years.

If you still find it hard to believe there is good evidence that it actually happened about six million years ago without any help from Herman Sörgel, although some of his ancestors may have been around at the time. The evidence comes from recent work showing that the modern Mediterranean is underlain by vast deposits of salt— all that remains of the original sea water.

Even more fantastic is the picture of what must have happened at the end of the period when the connection with the Atlantic was reopened. Water must have roared in, falling in a gigantic cascade of around 3,000 metres in height, a waterfall carrying more than 1,000 times the volume of Niagara, sufficient to counteract the annual evaporation and refill the empty basin. What a spectacle it must have been the greatest aquashow of all time and it is a sobering thought that there could have been ape-like men in the vicinity at the time.

In the contemporary spring, the spectacle from Tarifa, though not so awesome, is just as amazing. With mountains as a backdrop, the foreground is an admixture of wooded valleys, the trees going right up to the summits; on the lower slopes you can see a patchwork of irregular fields, each blocked out in its own particular pastel shade, pink, red, purple, blue, yellow even white. The fascinating thing is that the colour of each field is not always the result of the dominance of just one species of plant but often to admixtures of a number of plants each with similar coloured flowers. Just why they have become thus chromatically gregarious I don't know but certainly here is a case of multispecific colour bar.

It is well worth visiting the region of Tarifa just to see the painted fields, one of the true wonders of natural Spain. The

SOME OF THE FLOWERS WHICH PAINT THE FIELDS OF SPRING

		March	April	May	June
Pink	Lavatera trimestris (mallow)		●	●	●
	Malva hispanicus (mallow)		●	●	●
	Convolvulus althaeoides (bindweed)		●	●	●
	Ononis reclinata & other pink species Rest Harrow		●	●	
	Erodium cicutarium ssp. (forma primulaceum) (Storks Bill)	●	●	●	
Reddish	Fedia cornucopiae	●	●	●	
	Hedysarum glomeratum & H. coronarium		●	●	
	Rumex species (Docks)			●	●
Purple to Bluish	Galactites tomentosa (thistle)			●	●
	Centaurium erythraea ssp. grandiflora (magenta-pink)			●	●
	Echium lycopsis (Bugloss)		●	●	●
	Bourgaea humilis (thistle)			●	●
	Cleonia lusitanica (not every year, lilac)		●	●	
	Cerinthe major (iris)		●	●	
	Iris sisyrinchium (iris) massed mainly on roadsides		●	●	●
	Scabiosa atropurpurea, S. stellata & species (scabious)			●	●
	Convolvulus sicula, C. meonanthus (lilac or pinkish)		●	●	
Blue	C. tricolor (bindweed)		●	●	
	Anchusa azurea (blue bugloss)		●	●	
Yellow	Ridolfia segetum (like fennel)		●	●	
	Mustard		●	●	
	Dandelions & allied genera		●	●	
	Oxalis pes-caprae	●	●		
	Melilotus & Lotus spp. (field peas & trefoils)		●	●	
	Chrysanthemum segetum (Corn Marigold)		●	●	
	C. coronarium, C. myconis (chrysanthemums)	●	●	●	●
	Scolymus hispanicus (thistles)			●	●
	Euphorbia medicaginea (spurge)	●	●	●	
	Ranunculus spp. (buttercups)	●	●		
White	Asphodelus microcarpus (=aestivas) (ashpodel)	●	●		
	Anthemis, Chrysanthemum & allied genera	●	●	●	●
	Daucus carota (carrot)		●	●	●
	Ammi majus & other species, & other umbels			●	●
	Bellis annua (daisy)	●	●		
	Ranunculus spp. (covering ponds) (buttercups)	●	●	●	

time to do just that is some time between March and June, late
April early May being optimal, but of course only in a normal
year, too little or too much rain too early or too late can really
muck it all up. When you do go, be sure to take a hand lens so
that you can peer into the flowers and see the crab spiders in
all their pastel glory. These beautiful spiders have evolved to
be the same colour as the flowers in which they live, preying on
the visiting insects. They thus exhibit pastel protection in a
field of their own and in the punch up prior to each meal they
inadvertently help the process of pollination. The pastel
flowers themselves take up the opportunity of the rains of
spring, their seeds and other reproductive bodies lying dormant throughout much of the dry heat of the rest of the year.

Fig 36 *Crab spider satisfied with
his meal*

Once the Mediterranean as we now know it had filled up, the
contemporary pattern of climate was set. The area around
Tarifa is more exposed to the direct effect of the rain-bearing
westerlies, so much so that its rivers flow all year round, and
yet its summers are still hot and dry. It is in these river valleys
that much of the floristic magic of the area is to be found and
there is one person who knows an awful lot about it. Her name
is Mrs Betty Molesworth Allen, a British botanist, who has
lived in the area of Cadiz for many years with her husband an
ornithologist, who records the passing migrants in superb
photographs and films.

Perhaps a British botanist doesn't seem too out of place in
the shade of the mixed forests that form a gallery of cool green
in the valley bottoms. The light green spring leaves of the de-

ciduous oak *Quercus faginea* are very reminiscent of our own *Quercus petraea* as are the moss covered trunks and boulders, the admixture of Holly, Ivy and the delicate fronds of the Lady Fern looking not unlike green paper lace. The big regular green sweeps' brushes of the large horsetail *Equisetum telematei* makes one feel very much at home while the presence of the Royal, Maidenfern and Killarney ferns transports one in mind at least to the forests of Western Ireland. This certainly is the place to look for ferns; and I can guarantee that you won't be disappointed. The large stands of the Royal Fern with its dimorphic fronds, the majority of which consist of broad leaves compounded of flat segments or pinnules. These subtend the reproductive fronds which lack a leaf blade and consist only of masses of brown sporangia looking not unlike a withered leaf. Large as they may be, the Royal Fern is almost dwarfed by the fronds of *Culcita macrocarpa* which can reach a length in excess of 2 metres. This giant is, however, now getting rarer and rarer, not due to its massive leaves but to the fact that its hairy, part-underground stems are used in the manufacture of a local medicine. Another set of hairy rhizomes belong to the Hares Foot *Davallia canariensis* which, growing both on tree trunks and rocks, sheds its fronds in the dry weather; sleeping the summer through in a form which provides it with its common name, like a brown Hare resting in the sun.

The list of the ferns and their relatives which occur in the region is too long to allow full enumeration, but one more must be mentioned and that is *Psilotum nudum*. Very early on in the evolution of plants some group of plants must have taken the first step along the road towards a high and dry life on land. All the evidence points to the first footers as being members of a primitive group, the *Pteridophytes* which include all the ferns and their allies. The first fossils of these remarkable plants were found in a chert quarry, near the town of Rhynie in Scotland, where it had lived a semi-aquatic mode of life in a swamp some 400 million years before its discovery. It was soon realised that this first dry footing fossil had much in common with two plants which still grow abundantly in the damp warm forests of the tropics and sub-tropics by name of *Psilotum*. *Psilotum* is a very primitive plant consisting as it does of a dichotomously branched stem, bearing only tiny scale leaves. In the axes of some of these tiny leaves there are spore cases absolutely bursting with the spores of the next generation. The spore case splits into three parts, opening to expose the spores and thus releasing them to the atmosphere. *Psilotum* has much in common with the prototype land plants and so it is an exciting thing to find anywhere. It was in fact only very recently found growing in

Fig 37 *Psilotum nudum, a member of the Spanish flora*

Europe by Betty Allen, its nearest known locality being on the Cape Verde Islands way to the south.

One of the great fascinations of Tarifa is the fact that looking east there is the Mediterranean, an almost tideless sea which gives its name to a hot dry climate which spans the world; looking west there is the Atlantic, an ocean which reflects the full interplay of the movements of our nearest neighbours in space, in the incessant rise and fall of its tides. An ocean which affects the climate of the whole western fringe of Europe with its warm, water-laden winds. Somewhere out there to the west are the Azores, western outpost of Europe, clothed in what must be the most oceanic/atlantic vegetation of all.

Passing west from Tarifa the vegetation becomes richer in members of the Heather family and one can have the singular experience of seeing the Dwarf Palm alongside Ling and Prickly Pear on the margin of what is to all intents and purposes a wet heath. One plant well worth looking for is an insect-catcher, closely related to our Sundews, and called *Drosophyllum lusci-tanicum*. Its large yellow flowers give its presence away even from a distance and its elongate leaves are well armed with glandular hairs. These help in the digestion of the hapless insects, although they cannot, in fact, move to help to catch the prey. This insectivorous plant, unlike many of its relatives, likes to grow in dry stony places on acid rock and is confined to southern Spain and Portugal.

Here on the corner of the Iberian Peninsula the two climates, Oceanic and Mediterranean meet and mingle, bringing together a fabulous mixture of plants, enough to make a visiting botanist feel both at home and away, a feeling much enhanced by the ever presence of Gibraltar (GB). Apart from being an outpost of our sterling currency, it is also an outpost of limestone rock set in a sea of acid sandstones. Mt Algibe on the Spanish mainland rises to 1092 metres which, although a modest bulk compared to the high Sierras, is enough to squeeze considerable amounts of water out of the westerly winds bringing a certain lushness to the mouth of the Mediterranean.

The real rain of south west Spain however waters the western slopes of the Sierra Nevada, enriching the plain of Andalusia and the flow of its main river, the Guadalquivir, as it reaches the sea in the Gulf of Cadiz. The mouth of the river is a very exciting place for it was at the monastery of La Rabida that Christopher Columbus planned his voyages which opened up the promise of the New World to an overflowing Europe.

It was also nearby that the World Wildlife Fund had its beginnings. It's an organisation dedicated to save as much of the natural world as possible for the benefit of future generations

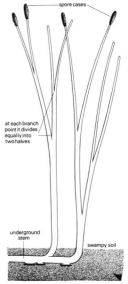

Fig 38 *Fossil of Rhynia, a prototype land plant*

of mankind, and also for the continuance of the process of evolution. Here they laid the plans to purchase the Coto Doñana as a permanent nature reserve covering some 6,500 hectares which have been described as the most important sanctuary for rare birds and mammals in Europe. Its area was extended in 1969 by the annexation of the Guadiamar Nature Reserve, the total of 35,000 hectares being given the status of a National Park.

It may seem ironical that the adjacent 21,000 hectares is a sporting reserve belonging to the Gonzalez Sherry Kings. Fortunately Don Mauricio Gonzalez is one of Spain's leading

Fig 39 Genetta Genetta, the genet, one of the highlights of the Coto Donana

Fig 40 The statuesque Lynx that welcomes you to the Coto Donana

Fig 41 The birthplace of the World Wildlife Fund

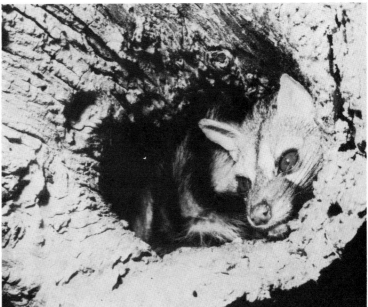

voices of conservation and the area is under his personal protection. It is all too easy to point the thoughtless finger of scorn at the regal guns of the past but it must be remembered that if it had not been for the long history of sporting interests in the region, who knows what the fate of these rich wetlands would have been. Drained to quasi-agriculture in all probability.

The Palacio, now headquarters of the National Park administration, was built in 1624 for the visit of King Felipe to the hunting reserve, or coto, owned by the Dukes of Medina and named after one of their wives, Doña Ana. They came each year to hunt the rich bird and animal life, just as today's visitors come to see and marvel at it. But why this richness? The coast-line between the mouth of the Rio Tinto and the Guadalquivir is an almost straight stretch of sandy beach backed by a magnificent series of sand dunes. The dunes of Arenas Gordas rise to over 60 metres in height. It is these dunes, built by the onshore winds, that impede the free drainage of the Guadalquivir, ponding back its waters to form extensive lagoons called the Marismas, which are thick with reedbeds and dotted with clay islands. An area difficult of access by man and thus affording protection for birds which come in their hundreds of thousands to rest or nest. The birds in turn provide food for a range of mammals including Spotted Lynx, Mongoose, Genets, Wildcat and Wild Boar and Red and Fallow Deer graze the rich meadows and Otters play in the water.

It's an ideal place to drain and turn over to agriculture with irrigation water on tap; an ideal place in which to develop a water-hungry industrial complex. The mind boggles at just what could have happened to it, perhaps it was better that the Dukes of Medina protected its potential, presenting the modern world with a ready-made reserve, whose immense value is now understood and, one hopes, is safe forever. Just how safe is that hope? That long straight beach and complex of shifting sand which are the creators of the Marismas, could well be their undoing. The beaches of the Costa del Sol are overflowing and the boom chalets of Portugal are booming their way down across the Algarve. Already the coast road has been extended and the new resort of Torre la Miguera overflows its holiday-makers into its stunted forest of Umbrella Pines. All we can do is hope that the voice of sensible long term planning will be heard, that further development will be minimised, enough and only enough to provide access for those who wish to come and see the natural treasures of this corner of Spain.

I know of no place better to sit and reminisce on the rapidly changing face of the world than on the highly mobile dunes of the Coto Donãna. The incessant movement of the great waves

Fig 42 *Shifting sands leave a Sea Thrift high and almost dry*

of sand, blown by the interplay of the winds, can bury mature pine trees so rapidly that only their topmost branches, still in leaf, protrude from the apex of the dune. A change in wind can likewise re-excavate the tree before it has been suffocated by the sand.

It is this ever changing but ever present pattern of dunes which has created this the wonderland of Europe in the mouth of a river which fortunately receives and retains more than its fair share of the rain that falls on Spain.

Fig 43 *Creeping dunes, death for some, new life for others*

The sea that lost its savour

Way up north, in the jumble of blue shapes which obscures the border between the Dancing Girl of Finland and the western edge of the great land mass that is Soviet Russia, there is a stretch of water that is absolutely clear—at least about its identity. It is neither a very large lake, nor a very deep lake, it does not house a mythical monster, nor is it the habitat of some rare species, in fact its only claim to fame is in its name *Jaurjärviosersee*.

Jaur means lake in Lappish, Järvi the same in Finnish, Osero means lake in Russian, while See is the German word, you've guessed it, for lake. Lake, lake, lake, lake is thus its proper name, the four variations on the theme recording the phases of occupation of this still remote area of Europe.

Of all the places in the world, Finland is perhaps the one that should be most careful, yet the most malleable, when labelling any area of water as a lake or a sea. There is no doubt that both should be baptised as 'water', the factor that is most often in doubt is their exact salt content.

Finland is a country that overflows with an estimated 55,000 lakes, that is one lake to every 100 members of the population and, as the majority of the lakes abound with islands, it would probably be true to say that every Finn could have his, or her, own bit of land on which to live in glorious isolation! Mind you, the glorious isolation would terminate each year as winter turned the water into ice.

Finnish lakes have two other striking features. Firstly, they are highly irregular in outline, often with long thin arms or embayments. In any one district all these arms are aligned in one direction which marks the movement of land ice during the last glaciation. Second, is the fact that the majority are shallow, the deepest on record being Kallavesi, plumbed at a mere 102 metres; and this leads to the greatest paradox of all. The total volume of fresh water stored in this, the land par excellence of lakes, is very small, being somewhere around 210 cu km, which would just about fill lake Vanern in Sweden.

Long, thin and shallow they may be, but they have provided Finland with a very beautiful landscape and an excellent and cheap system of internal transport; and this was one of the

factors in the early settlement of this otherwise rather alien land. For about six months the Finnish way is paved with the beauty of liquid water, and for six months with the same substance, but in solid form. So winter and water navigation are a must and form an important feature of the curricula of all Finnishing schools.

Apart from their size, shape and shallowness, the lakes of Finland abound with many other surprises, not the least being *Phoca hispida*, the freshwater, yes freshwater seal! Its ancestors used to live in the Arctic Ocean, from whence they migrated into the Baltic during the Ice Age. The enormous weight of the ice sheet lying across the land mass depressed Fennoscandia so much that the Baltic Sea was at one time much more extensive, covering much of the now lowest lying areas of Finland, including of course all those irregular lakes. As the ice melted, Finland heaved a sigh of relief and the land mass started to rise to the occasion. Gradually more and more of these arms of the sea were cut off from the mother Baltic, to become lakes which 'lost their savour', the salt diluted and flushed out by the melting ice and rain. In many of these new lakes, various populations of marine plants and animals must have been cut off. Those which could not adapt to the change in salinity, however gradual, were doomed to extinction; others with a more adaptable physiological nature survived and thrived in their new found isolation.

Although we always tend to think of seals as denizens of salt water they do, and often of their own accord, move into estuaries and up rivers. So, for the great, great, great, great grandmother *Phoca hispida* the change was not too much of a shock and her descendants, *Phoca hispida saimensis*, still live in Lake Saimaa, happy in the protection afforded to them by the new laws passed by the government of Finland. I don't know whether it is the feeling of protection or the fact that they are now sitting well above the salt, that has put the cheeky look on the face of this seal! Its nearest relatives, at least isotonically speaking, are *Phoca capsica* and *Phoca sibirica*. The first live it up in the Caspian, the second in Lake Baikal in Mongolia. These have been living in sweet-water isolation for a much longer period of time than the Baltic seal and have evolved into very distinctive looking animals. Who knows what is in store for the freshwater seal of the Baltic? Will evolutionary time confer on its elevated personage the distinction of *Phoca balticus*?

It is a surprising fact that, wherever you stand, sit or lie in Finland, you are gradually rising up in the world, because the land is still heaving its sigh, uplifting to produce its modern

Fig 44 *Lakescape Finnish style*

Fig 45 *Phoca hispida saimensis happy in the protection of new laws. Illustration by kind permission of Eric Bruun*

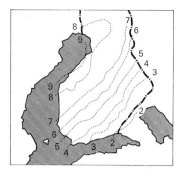

Fig 46 *High rise in Finland, the lines show the annual rise in millimetres*

relief. The greatest rate of contemporary uplift is, naturally, nearest the part which bore the greatest burden of ice, which is, or rather was, along the coast of the Gulf of Bothnia. Here the land is rising at the incredible rate of 90 cm a century and, although you can't exactly feel it, the rise is made manifest by the number of mooring rings, boat houses and even harbours that are now high and dry, well inland. Even the not-so-oldest inhabitants can reminisce about rowing and fishing on the exact spot on which you are now walking and talking; and it is said that Finland gains a new parish every hundred years. What a place for the real estate speculator! Finnish law, however, states that all the new lands are of common ownership and so the land sharks must console themselves with the fact that any high rise they construct will continue rising. (Freshwater seals yes, but land sharks impossible! Well, who knows with that rate of uplift?)

So the modern Baltic is a mere shadow of its former extent and is gradually shrinking as the unequal process of uplift continues and, as it shrinks, more and more bits get nipped off to form new lakes. A quick look at a map of the Baltic will make it quite clear that it is not only the new lakes that are changing, but that the Baltic itself is in danger of losing its savour.

The Baltic is the largest and best-known marine area in the world which enjoys a considerably lowered salinity. Its connection with the open ocean is tortuous, to say the least, the incoming water having to negotiate two right angled bends and some very narrow straits, namely the Great and Little Belt and, the narrowest of all, The Sound. Furthermore, the Baltic is surrounded by a vast land mass, which collects rain water, pouring it down to the land locked sea; added to this the whole area enjoys, if that is the right word, a climate in which there is very little loss of water due to evaporation, and so there is little or no concentration of the dilute waters.

The salt water entering the Skagerrak, pushed in by westerly winds, has a salinity of 35 parts per million, here in the narrowest straits it mixes with the outflow from the Baltic; the result is that the waters of the Kattegat average around 20 parts per million salt. Once past the Danish islands, the salinity is down to 8 parts per million. From here on, the change is very gradual 7, 6, 5, 4, 3 and even as low as 2 parts per million at the heads of both the Gulf of Bothinia and the Gulf of Finland.

It would thus be possible to position yourself, at least roughly, using a single instrument of navigation, one that is not usually found in ships chandlers – namely a salinometer. Salinometer design makes use of the fact that salt water conducts electricity much better than pure water, and so it can

provide the cruising biologist with a quick measure of the amount of salt in his aquatic environment. If you have the probe on a very long piece of wire, it is possible to measure the salinity down through the water body.

The proportion of salt dissolved in water also affects its density, so the higher the salinity the denser will be the water, which will sink to the bottom. It is for this reason that the deeper waters are more brackish. So my advice to all old salts who would make use of a salinometer to check their cruise around the Baltic is, 'never let your salinometer dangle too deep'.

However, there is no real need for a salinometer as long as you have a working knowledge of the local plants and animals because, in their own way, they are accurately sampling the saline environment. In fact, the distribution of certain plants and animals marked on a chart, provide a series of beacons with which your position, within the Baltic complex, can be determined with some accuracy.

The salinity nature trail of the Baltic reads something like this:—

Station 1. North Sea. Salinity 35 ppm.
Fifteen sorts of Sea Anemones, fifteen sorts of Sipunculid Worm, thirteen Chitons, seventy different sorts of Starfish, Brittlestars, Urchins and Sea Cucumbers. None of these are found within the Baltic proper.

Station 2. Odense. (Hans Christian Andersen born here.)
Salinity 15 ppm. All the above animals becoming rare, few seaweeds or Marine Sponges present, Octopi and Squids absent.

Station 3. Bornholm. Salinity 7 ppm.
Kelp still present, also the Lugworm, *Arenicola* and the Winkle, *Littorina littorea* are present on the shore.

Station 4. Gotland. Salinity 6 ppm.
The last of the Kelp is found here in the deeper, more saline water. Of the 330 odd Amphipods that are found back in the North Sea, only twelve species can be found as far up as this.

Station 5. Tvärminne. Salinity 5 to 6 ppm.
This is a real must for all visiting biologists, easily reached from the capital, it houses the marine biological station of the University of Helsinki. The Director is a botanist by the name of Hans Luther and a walk along the shore or, better still, a row out in a boat with Dr Luther as your guide is an experience which will never be forgotten.

Looking down into the water there is an admixture of plants enough to give any unprepared ecologist a nasty dose of the 'osmotic pressures'. Masses of Bladderwrack grow in the sheer luxuriance of the calm waters, interspersed with the long

Opposite Page

Top
The tide that never came back, high and dry at Vasa
(Chapter Five)

Bottom left
Stuck above the Stucco, Campanula pyramidalis
(Chapter Six)

Bottom right
Show us your Mussels. Doge City in the distance (Chapter Six)

Fig 47 Bellamy's
Baltic Nature Trail

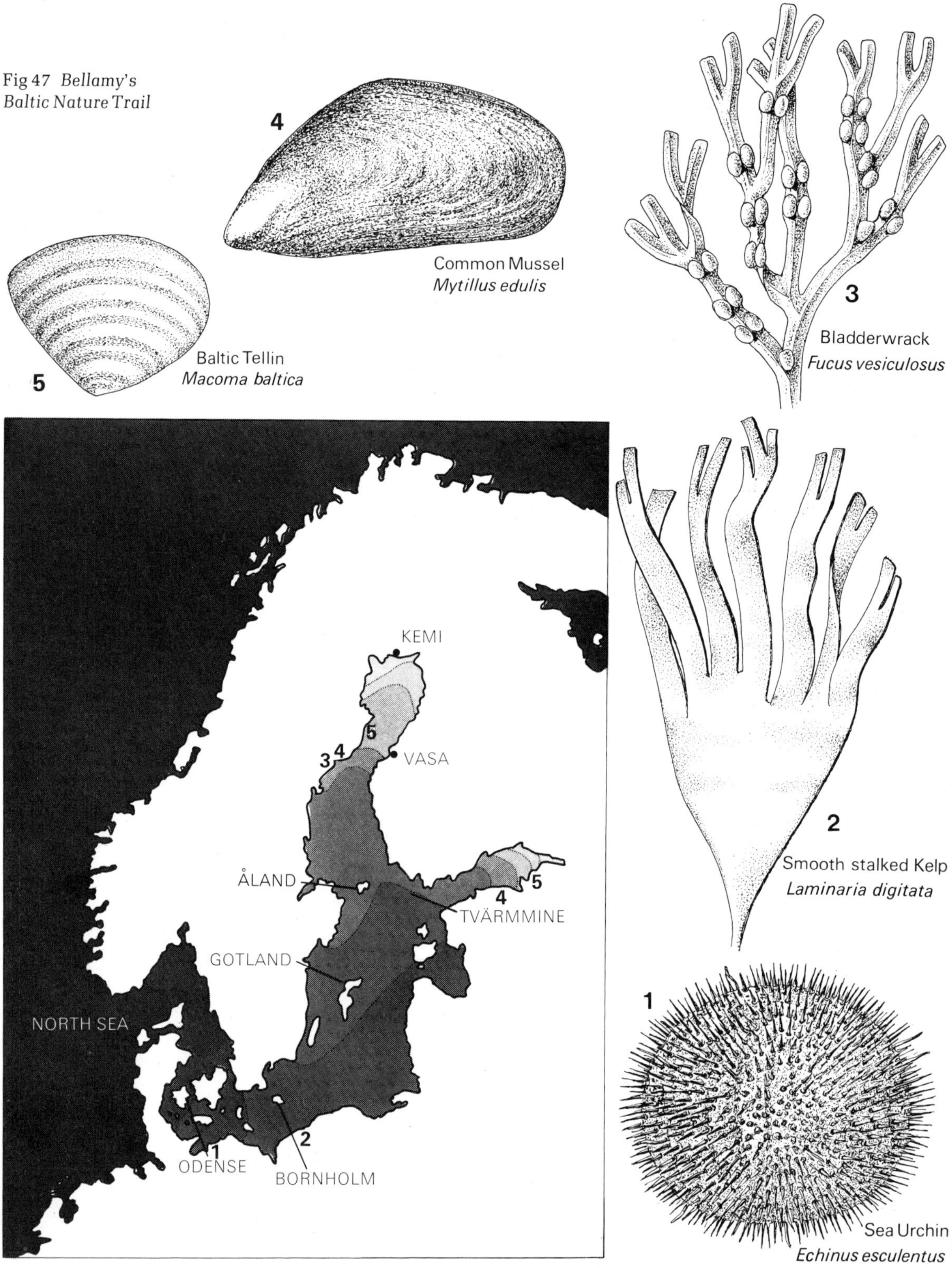

4

Common Mussel
Mytillus edulis

3

Bladderwrack
Fucus vesiculosus

5

Baltic Tellin
Macoma baltica

KEMI

5

3 **4**

VASA

2

Smooth stalked Kelp
Laminaria digitata

ÅLAND

4 **5**

TVÄRMMINE

GOTLAND

NORTH SEA

1

2

1

ODENSE

BORNHOLM

Sea Urchin
Echinus esculentus

66

strands of the Bootlace Weed, *Chorda filum*. Nothing to worry about, this is the Baltic Sea alright and they are seaweeds. But what are those masses of white flowers protruding above the surface? They belong to the Water Buttercup. A quick count of the heads of fruits shows more than forty and thus it is probably *Ranunculus baudotii*. In England this is a plant of brackish ditches near the coast, but not a denizen of the open sea. A flotilla of Common Jellyfish float by, although one must be careful with the name, for here they are only common when the wind is blowing in the right direction. This is one species that is certainly at its limit, its breeding success being absolutely dependent on the salinity of the water in which it lives. The adults have always been a well known feature of the Baltic, even right up into the Gulf of Bothnia. However, their success in breeding has, in the past, been limited to areas south and east of Hango, although small rises in salinity have allowed successful breeding around Tvärminne in recent years.

The research station at Tvärminne is a world centre for research into the adaptation of both plants and animals to the effect of reduced salinity. Recently, detailed work has been carried out on the Viviparous Blenny, a fish which retains its eggs internally and 'lays' its young all alive oh. The work has shown that the embryos develop safe within mum, bathed in their own private swimming pool which has a salinity not unlike that of the North Sea. They are common members of the inshore fish fauna around Tvärminne and one can only guess that their birth must be quite a shock, at least in saline terms.

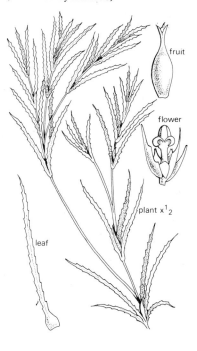

Fig 48 *Najas marina* L
(*so named by Linneus*)

Yes, the Baltic is a place to shock most biologists brought up in the big, unconfined world of the open ocean, a place where one could perhaps be forgiven for making mistakes! Even the great Karl Linneus himself, Swedish naturalist par excellence and the man who dreamed up the now universally accepted system of binomial nomenclature (the correct naming of all plants and animals), made a grave mistake and all because of the Baltic Sea. He first described and named the plant *Najas marina*. 'Oh no!' said the pundits, '*Najas* is a genus which is only found in fresh water. Its abundance in the Baltic Sea around Tvärminne vindicates the Swedish maestro, although it doesn't help to clarify the question 'when is a sea not a sea?'

Station 6. The Islands of Åland. Salinity 5 ppm.
Bladderwrack is still present although not as abundant from here northwards, in fact, from here on, the plant retreats downwards with the saltier water, becoming smaller and more 'miserable' looking. Similarly with the Mussel and the Barnacle, *Balanus improvisus*, they are both present at Åland, but are beginning to feel the dearth of the salt.

Perhaps this is the place to stop, take a rest from natural history and go on a fishing trip! My advice is 'don't', especially if you are Ichthyologically inclined, ie, if you know anything about fish. A fishing trip can result in a catch of a really mixed up nature. Bream, Pike, Perch and Trout, all denizens of fresh water, can be caught along with Baltic Herring, Lavaret and Cod, all swimming in the same lake, sea? – ah well, does it really matter?

Station 7. Vasa. Salinity 5/4 ppm.

Here Bladderwrack finds its saline limit, as does the Common Mussel. Here *Phragmites*, the Reed grows out into the shallow embayment of the sea and the Cows of Vasa come to graze on its succulent shoots and on the other predominantly freshwater weeds. It is not an unusual sight to see the whole herd take a short cut by swimming across an arm of the sea. In this way they keep the weight off their hooves and the Mosquitoes from their soft under parts, because from here up the sea is a breeding ground for the Mosquito.

While filming near Vasa our host was Mauri Palomarki, Rector of Vasa University and Professor of Economic Geography. His knowledge of the local flora was absolutely phenomenal, although on many occasions he apologised that he had forgotten most of it as he had done no botany since his undergraduate days. He has also a fund of stories and, as we stood on a bed of common reed, he recounted one that I shall never forget.

The Devil once challenged God to a contest to see who could make the best plant. God made the Coconut Palm (*Cocos nucifera*) and the Devil made the Common Reed (*Phragmites australis*). The Devil's plant prospered and spread to many watery spots throughout the world while God's Coconut Palm did well, but stayed staunchly within the tropics. 'I've won,' claimed the Devil. 'No,' said God, 'now we must put the plants to their final test, climb up to the top of your plant.' As the Devil sank beneath the water he gnashed his teeth in rage biting two pieces out of the base of the leaf. If you look very carefully, you can still see them today.

Now this story got me looking and I reckon that the Devil's Tooth Marks are not nearly as deep on the British population of *Phragmites* as they are on the Reeds which grow in Finland. I have no proof, perhaps its just an impression, it is however one I am going to look into more carefully.

As you go about Britain and especially about Europe keep close watch on the commonest and most widespread plants you encounter, you may be surprised at the range of variation. Mind you, you shouldn't be too surprised, take a look at your

Fig 49 The cows of Vasa, udders below the water but above the salt

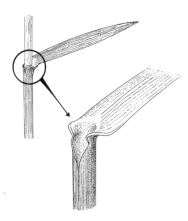

Fig 50 Devil's Toothmarks

fellow human beings, and they are all the same species, *Homo sapiens forma europaeus*, what a range of form.

Of all the places on the salinity trail it is Vasa which should remind us most of the factor for which we must be thankful. One of the animals which low salinity has excluded from the Baltic is *Teredo*, the Shipworm. It is for this reason that many of the wooden ships of various lines which sank in the Baltic are still there, almost intact, safe from this, one of the only products of evolution able to digest wood. The Vasa is the most famous of these unbored wrecks, and it is now, raised, restored and replaced in its home port of Stockholm.

Station 8. Kemi. Salinity 3/2 ppm.

The salt has almost gone and with it the most stalwart of the marine animals, *Macoma*, the Baltic Tellin. Kemi is one of the main ports of the northern Baltic and its industry shows that, although the Shipworm is not a part of the Baltic scene, there is another animal that lives, or at least makes its living out of wood, and its name is *Homo sapiens* var. *finlandicus*.

Finland is one of the world's major exporters of wood and wood products; for example, in 1970 this small country produced 6·3% of the world's woodpulp. The wood is brought from the forest along the waterways to the Baltic and from there its products are exported worldwide. The only problem is that, between November and May, the ports are closed by ice, for it is a fact that fresh water freezes at a higher temperature than salt water. Added to this is the problem of pollution of an enclosed sea; the sweet water can rapidly be turned very sour, especially close to large pulp works and sawmills.

Concern has been shown in recent years over the build up of oxygen deficiency in some of the deep parts of the Baltic. The accusing finger has pointed at both the industrial and domestic organic waste that pours down into the deep and increases the rate of utilisation of dissolved oxygen. More detailed study has, however, shown that these pools of oxygen deficiency are by no means static, nor are they purely recent phenomena. There is, in fact, every indication that, long before industrial man arrived on the Baltic scene, there were pools of oxygen deficiency in some of the deeps. At irregular intervals great 'pistons' of oxygen rich salt water are forced into the Baltic and they flush out the 'dead' water and stir up the nutrients, refreshing the sea.

It is certainly a very complex picture and man is accentuating certain of its worst aspects. For this reason, all the nations who empty their waste waters into the Baltic have got together and agreed to limit their polluting activities, and to monitor the health of this land-locked sea.

Of the 337,000 sq km that is Finland, 32,000 sq km are covered with water or ice, depending on the time of year, and another 110,000 sq km are covered with water in another form, to be exact peat. Water is liquid water, ice is solid water and peat is water bound up in a matrix of partially decayed organic matter, mainly of plant origin. If wood is Finland's main resource, then peat must run as a very close second.

Just as the distribution of the aquatic plants and animals can be used to locate you within the Baltic, so too can the types of peatland (henceforth called 'mires') help locate your position on this very wet land. The only trouble is that it is best done from the air, because mires are often of such gigantic extent that it is difficult to comprehend them from ground level. However, Finnair run a super fly-about-as-you-please, all-in ticket which must be designed especially for peatnicks!

Fig 51 *Aapa mire from the air (above)*

Fig 52 *Palsa mire, a lump of frozen peat*

Zone 1 The mires of the first zone have very little character even when viewed from the air. They fill all the basins, both large and small, and the surface of many of them are being colonised by trees from their margins inward.

Zone 2 The mires of this zone are very distinctive features, being readily picked out from the air due to the fact that their surface is marked with concentric rows of small pools which circle the highest point of the mire system.

Zone 3 These mires look not unlike those of the last zone, but the pools are arranged excentrically, again around the highest point of the mire surface. The reason for the excentricity is that these mires actually grow on the sides of valleys and hence the highest point of the peat mass is usually near the top.

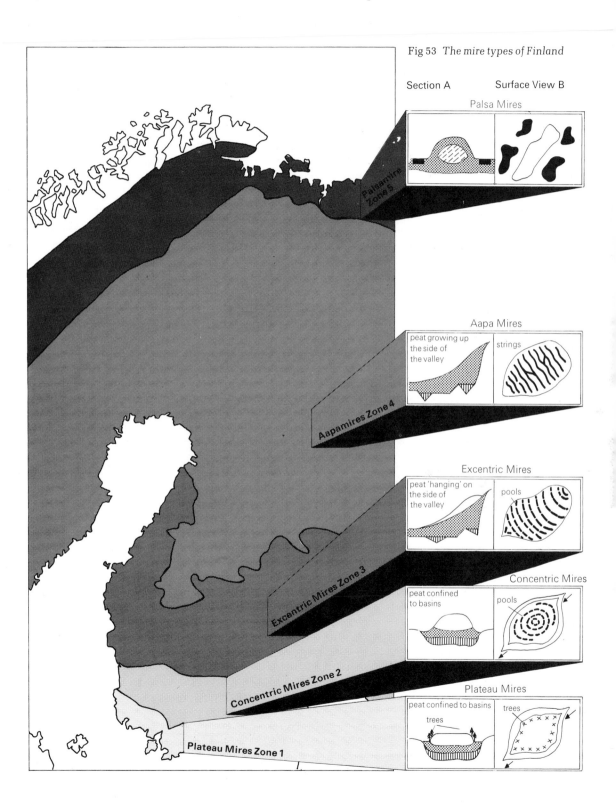

Fig 53 *The mire types of Finland*

Section A   Surface View B

Palsa Mires

Palsamires Zone 5

Aapa Mires

peat growing up the side of the valley   strings

Aapamires Zone 4

Excentric Mires

peat 'hanging' on the side of the valley   pools

Excentric Mires Zone 3

Concentric Mires

peat confined to basins   pools

Concentric Mires Zone 2

Plateau Mires

peat confined to basins   trees

trees

Plateau Mires Zone 1

Fig 54 *A trio of Brown Mosses*

Fig 55 *Greenland Tea*

Zone 4 This contains the commonest mire type to be found in Finland and they are so abundant that there is a word for them in the Finnish language. The word is 'Aapa'; and Aapa Mires are often gigantic, covering large areas on the sides of shallow valleys, fed by water draining down from the catchment..They are very easy to recognise from the air because their surface consists of elongate pools called flarks, separated by equally elongate peat ridges that go under the name of strange, of strings.

The strings are built up almost entirely of the Brown Bog Moss, *Sphagnum fuscum*, and they form a series of 'coffer dams', lying across the surface slope, hence impeding the flow of surface water down across the mire expanse. They are covered with a tangle of heathy plants, Bog Rosemary, Cow berry, Crowberry and Bog Ledum, to name but a few. These live it up on the drier, higher strings, out of the way of the water which flows its tortuous way through the flarks. The flowing water brings with it a supply of minerals, originally dissolved from the catchment, and these help feed and nourish the plants. The vegetation of the flarks is very different from that of the strings, being dominated by a whole range of sedges, including the Many Flowered Bog Cotton, set against a background of brown mosses. These include the juicy Scorpion Moss, *Scorpidium scorpioides*, the starry *Campylium stellatum* and the feather-like perfection of *Cratoneuron commutatum*. Sorry about the Latin names but, to the expert, each one tells something about the environment of that part of the flark in which it is found.

Fig 56 *Bog Rosemary*

Fig 57 *Crowberry*

Fig 58 *Cowberry*

The Aapa Mires really are the most fabulous places in which to wet your feet and whet your appetite for Arctic plants. It is in the flarks that the Reindeer make their awkward way to feed and drink, obtaining from the luxuriance of the vegetation sufficient calcium to enable them each year to produce a new set of antlers. I reckon that the Aapa Mires are one of the natural wonders of the world, especially in autumn when the festive yellow/red of the leaves of the Dwarf Birch pick out the margins of the sinuous flarks.

The real problem of the Aapa Mire country is how to get about. In order to do it dry shod, you must stick to the strings; they are not the easiest things to walk about on and the journey to the next dry spot, down or up slope, can be tortuous in the extreme. Difficult as it is for us humans, and come to that, even for the reindeer who have the advantage of a leg at each corner, to get about, it must be 'murder' for something as small as an ant. Nevertheless, one of the most striking features of the strings are great bald mounds protruding from among the dwarf shrubs; these are the nests of the Wood Ant. How is it that they make their way along the strings in order to collect the conifer needles to make their nests? Close inspections of the nest will reveal the fact that they have learned to live with the problem in a very practical way. The nest mounds are constructed from Ledum leaves which abound on their long island homes.

Zone 5 If the Ants can, and ever do, look out from the tops of their nests, they would be able to see a series of gigantic mounds which would probably make them feel rather jealous. They range from ant hill dimensions up to and beyond those of the average burial barrow. Again, they are such common landscape features that the locals call them Palsas. Close inspection reveals that they are made of peat and the peat is being made of

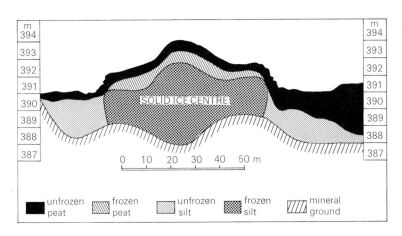

Fig 59 *Section of a palsa mound in summer*

Sphagnum fuscum. From the top of a big Palsa you can see way out over the Park Tundra, with its scattered copses of Birch trees, the streams picked out by the brighter greens of the willow thickets.

The real secret of the Palsas is, however, hidden below ground. Each living Palsa has a hard core of solid ice. Throughout the winter these singular mounds of peat are frozen solid right up to their icy surface. Raised as they are, well above the general surface of the surrounding terrain, they will not be covered by a deep blanket of snow and so the winter frosts will penetrate very deep. As the spring turns to Arctic summer, the Palsas begin to melt from the outside in, the melt waters providing the Bog Mosses with all the water they require for their growth. The summers are short and, long before the hard core completely melts, it is autumn again and re-freeze gets under way.

The hard centres of the Palsa Mires are the first sign of permafrost in the Arctic landscape. Further north, there is a great sheet of Permafrost which circles the northern hemisphere. To tread this magic deep frozen terrain, one of course has to turn right and head for the real tundras of Russia. Permafrostwise the palsas are as far as one can go in Finland. Not far away is the Arctic Ocean and, of course, somewhere up there is Spitzbergen, northern outpost of Eurasia.

Doge city

The Roman Empire was crashing around the laurel wreaths of the Caesars, the great civilisation was doomed and, out of that sea of trouble, Venice arose, an island refuge for the dying culture. The year was AD 42. At first it was no more than a lake village, not unlike those of the Bronze Age, built on wooden stilts safe above the waterlogged silt of 117 tiny islets. Safe on their island refuge, the Venetians elected their first Doge in AD 697 and, from that time on, grew in strength and commercial supremacy until they controlled much of the Eastern Mediterranean.

The bulk of the Venice depicted on the incredibly expensive picture postcards and captured on the millions of 'appy 'oliday snaps taken every year, that great mass of crumbling grandeur, was piled up, or is the word shored up, during the 400 years which span the fourteenth to eighteenth centuries. Wherever you walk in Venice, not too far away beneath your overheated feet is one of over 22 million wooden stakes, the majority of which are as sound as the day they were driven into the soft silts of the lagoon. The reason for their long non-rotting service is that the lagoon muds are, and presumably always have been, deficient in oxygen.

As you float about in your gondola or evaporate in your vaporetto, take a look at the tide line around the bases of the great mooring posts. Amid the thick clusters of Mussels there are definite signs of decay, in fact many of the posts, even in the Grand Canal, are now so far gone that even the Mussels are losing their moorings. The reason for this extra bit of decaying grandeur is that the surface waters do become charged with oxygen, both from photosynthesis by the plant plankton and from the turbulence caused by all the propellors of the motor boats that rush up and down. Fortunately, the piles on which the city actually stands are usually way down out of this particular sphere of influence, stalwart in their deoxygenated muds.

One of my favourite pastimes in any city is to find a hole in the ground, you know – one of those where you can stand at your ease and watch other people at work! The great fascination of Venetian holes in the ground is that they often reveal the original wooden piles, each of which can be extracted with a lugubrious sucking plop up into the light of the twentieth century. Once cleaned up, these lignified Rip Van Winkles each has its own particular story to tell because, in the pattern of their annual rings, there is a record of the annual weather cycle over the years of their growth. The art of interpreting these post dated weather records forms the basis of the science of Dendrochronology, the main requisites for which are a lot of patience and a good idea of the origin of the trees from which the posts were made. Then, with a little bit of help from radio-carbon dating, you are in a business which makes giant jig-saw puzzles look like tiddly-winks! The pattern of rings on your most recently acquired pile has to be compared and fitted in with all the other information in your data log, and so it goes on. The ideal is to obtain wood from a whole series of trees whose life spans overlapped, thus giving you a continuous record of the local climate of the forest from which they were cut.

One of the main problems of the dendrochronology of Venetian piles is that they didn't all come from the same place. The earliest piles were probably of local origin, Alder and, per-haps, Poplar from the shores of the lagoon itself, but Venice was to become the centre of a new and bustling commerce and, as that evolved, wood was culled from a wider area, Spruce from the mountain forests of the Dolomites and Oak and Alder from the coastal ranges of Yugoslavia, each new locality adding its own problem to the puzzle of the growth rings. Difficult as it may be to extract, remember it is there, not far beneath your feet one of the biggest stores of environmental data anywhere in the world.

As your gondolier manouvres around one of those ever-so-tight corners, reach out and remove a Mussel from the tide line, try and get a dead one if you can because the shells will make a good souvenir of your visit. A quick look at the pointed end of the shell will show you that this is not the common Edible Mussel, *Mytillus edulis*, which is found all around the British coast. It is, in fact, another species *Mytillus galloprovincialis* which, although present in Britain is mainly confined to our warmer south western coastlines. Mussels are suspension feeders, which means that they feed on organic matter sus-pended in the sea water which they continuously draw through their shells. The canals of Venice are full of excellent mussel-food, organic matter mainly of human origin, held in suspen-sion by the ebb and flow of the tide. This is one reason why *Mytillus galloprovincialis* (there's another one I can't pro-nounce) is such an abundant feature of the Venetian tide line. They hang there, living it up on all the good 'nosh' which flows into the canals at the convenience of the passing tourists; and that is why you must never, no never, eat mussels culled fresh from the canals of Doge City! If you do it may well be a case of 'see Venice and die', or at least spend most of your holiday in the sick bay rather than the lido.

Fig 60 *Know your mussels?*

THE POINTS TO REMEMBER

Mytillus edulis

Umbo at tip of the shell

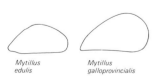

Mytillus edulis

Mytillus galloprovincialis

Best to leave them where they are, for one reason, their serried ranks act as ideal mini breakwaters, adding at least some protection to the crumbling stucco from the onslaught of the wake of the water taxis. Yes, life down at the water line is almost as crowded as San Marco at the height of the tourist boom for, apart from the myriad Mussels and Barnacles, each building and quayside is fringed with an edging of bright green mainly consisting of the two seaweeds *Enteromorpha intestinalis* and *Cladophora glomerata*, both of which choose to live in water which we fastidious humans have labelled as thoroughly polluted.

To the visiting biologist, Venice stinks of pollution, although I have never found the air as unsavoury as some reports make it out to be. The smell which permeates the city is, to me, of dank decay; and only when the bottom of one of the small dead-end canals is churned up does one smell the unmistakeable aroma of sewage.

Nevertheless, however sensitive your nose may be, both you (sorry, us) tourists and the local inhabitants should rejoice in the fact that the waters of Venice are indeed polluted. All the time there is excess organic matter pouring through the canals, the water will be bung full of bacteria thriving on the products of decay and, in so doing, using up the oxygen dissolved in the water and that helps to protect the all important piles.

In the not too distant past Venice was known as the Green City for then, not only did the campos and piazettas overflow with trees and other plants, but many of the largest palaces each had their gardens which, though ultra formal in layout, were bung full of chlorophyll. So it was that each day when the sun rose above the shimmering waters of the lagoon, the green lungs of Venice were switched on to pour out oxygen into the still air.

Today many of the gardens are no more and most of the campos are devoid of plant life, except for a few struggling Grasses, which are beaten into submission by the tramp of passing feet, all following the signs which seem to point, so haphazardly both to San Marco and the Piazza Roma. Many of the struggling weeds derive their water from underground tanks often as large as the campo itself, the tanks are, in turn, fed from the rain that gutters down from the buildings. In the past these same cisterns provided the Venetians with their only supply of sweet water, and the elaborate well heads which grace many of the squares are not, in fact, wells at all, simply points of access to the cisterns of the past.

Doge City is no longer green, and measurement has shown that, on a still night, the air in some of the alleys may become

Fig 61 *Formal Venice*

depleted of oxygen. The same must, of course, have happened in the past because plants, like animals, respire – using up oxygen in the process, so, in the absence of light, the plants themselves would put a drain on the oxygen stores of the still night air.

There is, of course, absolutely nothing to worry about, even under the very worst conditions, there is still plenty of oxygen down at ground level to supply even the most active bunch of tourists rushing about as only the tourists do in Venice. Nevertheless, walking about the pavements of the city one can feel further away from plant life than just about anywhere else in Europe. Yet, if you keep your eyes well open you can, with diligence, find a surprising variety of plants tucked away in the vastness of the city, not in the gardens but self sown and that is as wild as Venetian plants come.

La Flora Urbica di Venetzia published in 1975, lists no less than 147 vascular plants all of which grow 'wild' within the city limits. Included in this number are seven Ferns and twenty Grasses, the remainder belonging to forty-four families of the Flowering Plants. The book is the result of a lifetime of dedicated study by Professor Alesandro Marchello, the flora itself the result of many lifetimes of comings and goings by many millions of people to and from this world centre of commercial activity.

I don't know whether I have inadvertently carried any seeds with me on my various visits to Venice, but I do know that, in all my wanderings around the city, I have only managed to see a mere forty-two members of the urban flora.

The original flora of the islets on which the modern city has evolved must have consisted in the main of salt-loving plants, their roots immersed in the silts of the lagoon and their heads hardly raised above high tide level. As the city rose up upon its stilts, new habitats were formed on which real land-lubbers could survive and thrive; and one of the first of these plants was possibly *Campanula pyramidalis l.* The native home of this very handsome bellflower is far away in Istria; and legend has it that its seeds came to Venice with the building stone that was imported from the quarries of that region.

Fig 62 *Green lung on the Grand Canal*

The method of building was to drive the piles safe into the deoxygenated mud, cap them with a lattice of wooden planks and then add course after course of bricks in order to bring the non rot foundations up to the surface of the lagoon. Next was added a good thick chunk of Istrian stone, which effectively sealed off the rest of the building from the water beneath, a damp course in the classical style. With the damp course came the Pyramidal Bellflower and it still grows in abundance in some parts of the city, sprouting from wall tops, canal sides and even decorating the highest pinnacles of some of the churches.

If you ever do manage to find one of these tall stately Bellflowers growing down near the ground (and there is a trattoria behind the Campo Santa Fosca where the pasta is excellent and the owner has cultivated some beside his front door) then take a look into the top of the handsome blue bell of the flower. Most Bellflowers are strongly protandrous, which means that the pollen is often shed while the flower is still in bud, where it gets trapped amongst all the hairs that cover the long style and remains, ready to brush off on any passing insect.

And so it would appear that self-pollination must often be the order of the day. This is however not true because many of the Bellflowers are self-incompatible. This means that the pollen which is derived from the flowers of one plant are not effective when it comes to pollinating the flowers of the same plant. Complicated isn't it, and that is not the end of the story of pollination in the crafty *Campanulaceae*. If the pollen of one species of Bellflower gets to the stigma of another species while

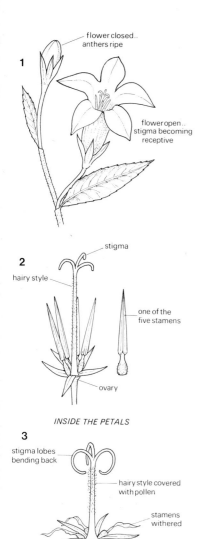

flower closed..
anthers ripe

1

flower open..
stigma becoming
receptive

stigma

2

hairy style

one of the
five stamens

ovary

INSIDE THE PETALS

3

stigma lobes
bending back

hairy style covered
with pollen

stamens
withered

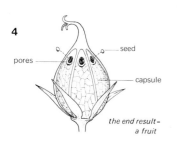

4

pores

seed

capsule

*the end result –
a fruit*

Fig 63 *Bellflower pollination*

it is in a receptive state then some kind of chemical warfare may ensue. The pollen tube of the foreign species either cannot grow or only grows very slowly. So it is that the pollen tube from another individual of the same species will always get to the ovule first. True love will always win, well at least 99·99 times out of 100 and the sanctity of the species will thus be maintained.

There is little likelihood that this incompatibility mechanism will ever be summoned into action by the Venetian populations of *Campanula pyramidalis* because this is the only species of bellflower present in the city. Or is it? There are, in fact, some 300 other Bellflowers, each waging their intimate chemical warfare, in the north temperate regions and on cool mountain slopes of the tropics; and I have a sneaking feeling that, behind the high walls and locked gates, there may be others waiting to get out to swell the ranks of the 147 members of La Flora Urbica.

In order to regale yourself with the botanical delights of Venice, you must keep your eyes open and not be too bashful to peer round corners, up at parapets and down into the dingiest of nooks and crannies. Mind you, you won't look too out of place, because most of the other visitors are going through the same performance, in search of inscriptions proclaiming exactly where Wagner wrote Lohengrin, or looking at some particular beastly stone carving. Venice is full of stone animals and most of 'em seem to be eating something. So, as I go looking for my plants I can brush up my gastronomic zoology, although the best way to do that is to sample the best of Frittura Mista at one of the canal-side restaurants.

There is a super one just beside the Rialto Bridge, whose table d'hôte reads like a zoology textbook and, if you don't fancy thinking about from exactly which phylum the melody of tastes originate, then you can always gaze at the bridge and ponder on the fact that its elegant bulk is held up by a mere 6,000 piles!

To see even a cross section of the plants you must, however, shun the bright lights of the Grand Canal and turn into the maze of fondamentos, rivas, sotto-porticos, campiellas and piazzettas which produce an amazing criss cross pattern of microclimates, varied and always varying as the sun swings across the cloudless sky. It is down in the cool depths and around the most shaded corners that one of the greatest surprises of your Venetian tour is to be found, and it doesn't even get a mention in most of the guide books. *Adiantum capillus veneris*, the seemingly ever-so-delicate Maidenhair Fern, a rare plant of shady nooks and crannies on the warmer, wetter coasts of Britain. So, what's it doing in dry old Venice? Come to

Fig 64 *Microclimates of Venice as seen from above*

think of it, it can't be all that delicate because it is a regular and stalwart member of that most ill-treated of world floras, the potted plants that you left unwatered when you locked up at home and took off for Europe! It will be waiting for your return, maybe a bit shrivelled, but after that quick post-holiday soak in the bathtub, it will be as good as new. So too, the Maidenhair Ferns of Venice live in the dark corners, waiting for the rains of spring to allow the completion of their complex life cycle which brings on another generation of long-suffering ferns.

No, don't just walk over the humpy dumpy bridge, and there's hundreds to choose from, peer down over the parapet and see whether you can discover this not-so-delicate Fern. If you do find it and the ones on that side are all withered and dried up, indulge yourself in a bit of microclimatology, rush to the other side, for there, sheltered from the direct rays of the sun throughout the day, it may be doing a lot better.

Apart from bargaining with the water taximasters, there are two other absorbing games to play when in Venice, but both must be played from a boat, the best type being – you've guessed – a gondola. The first is to take stock of the micro-climate of the canal and guess what plants will be growing on the far side of the next bridge. The second is a sort of Pooh Sticks in reverse. As you approach a bridge, each person in the boat selects a tourist and sees which one gets to the other side first to see you come out.

In all my floating about the canals, there is one plant for which I have searched in vain and that is the Common Reed. It used to be common in some of the backwater canals which, due to their accumulation of rubbish, were shut off from the main effects of the sea. Not only did it grow in abundance but it was also of great importance, for a bundle of its dry stalks provided torches to melt the pitch that blackened and caulked the bottoms of the canal boats. In recent years it has disappeared from the canals, because more regular clearance allows the tide to sweep right through the maze of waterways. Today, the only place I have seen it growing is in the wilder parts of that rambling car park where, each day, so many tourists spend happy hours searching for the exact spot in which they left their car.

Most visitors first step onto the promised land at the steps of the Piazza San Marco, and note well that this is the only Piazza in the whole of Venice, all the rest are of baser rank and only deserve the diminutive 'Piazzetta'; thank goodness for school Latin! As they land, their eyes are on the Doge's Palace and few even notice the yellow heads of the Rock Samphire growing along the edge of the canal. *Crithmum maritimum* is usually a plant of sea cliffs and, as the Doges omitted to build any, this handsome Umbellifer has come to terms with the situation and has taken to the mini cliffs of San Marco.

I cannot deny that I like St Mark's Square and all it has to offer. If you are lucky you may see Ivy Leaved Toadflax on the Bridge of Sighs and Groundsel on the parapets of the Basilica, but these come and go from year to year. I turn my steps towards the Madonna dell' Orto, where I know that *Campanula pyramidalis* will be waiting to remind me of all that imported stone from Istria, there keeping the city safe above the twice daily oscillation of the tide.

Perhaps one of the most surprising aspects of the Venetian scene is the plethora of tide marks, or indeed that there is any tide at all. The Adriatic is an almost tideless sea and yet on quite an ordinary day, floating about the canals, you will be aware of a rise and fall of at least one metre, the bottom half thereof picked out by the slime of weed and tassels of Mussels, the upper part by discoloration of the fascia. High spring tides can double the range and, if the winds are in the wrong direction and there has been rain up in the Venetian hills, the city may be in for real trouble as the water rises and gondolas can float right up to the Basilica San Marco. The problem is that the lagoon opens on to the Adriatic through three very narrow gaps and, if the conditions are wrong, the whole tidal flow gets bottled up with the river water and – well, it happened in 1966. To this add the fact that the city has, in recent years, been sinking and it looks as if the problem is here to stay, unless someone comes up with the right answer.

This whole tidal problem is manifest by the highest tide mark of all, some three metres up the affected buildings. The plain

Fig 65 *Phragmites australis, the common Reed, no longer so in Venice*

fact is that, once the water is over the top of the damp course, the bricks just soak it up by capillary action where, reaching its zenith it evaporates, leaving the stucco encrusted with salt. Recent study has blamed the sinking of Venice on the massive extraction of ground water, which has in consequence been banned, but only time will tell.

Unfortunately, Venice is not only in trouble from below, it

is also under attack from above. When the wind is blowing in the wrong direction, and that is west, from the industrial conglomerations of Mestre and Marghera, it is not too difficult to smell the trouble in the air of Doge City. It is enough to make even the eyes of the stone giants at the top of the staircase of the Doge's Palace weep green tears. They may well have protected the secrets of La Doga for more than four centuries, but they are now under attack from Venice's most insidious of enemies – sulphur dioxide. Sulphur dioxide (SO_2) is fortunately a very light gas and much of it escapes; unfortunately, it is also very soluble and when it rains, it dissolves to form a dilute solution of sulphuric acid (H_2SO_4) and the rain falls down onto calcium carbonate ($Ca.CO_3$).

> Johnny finding life a bore, swallowed H_2SO_4,
> Johnny's father, an MD gave him $CaCO_3$.
> Now he's neutralised that's true,
> But he's full of CO_2.

The trouble is that much of the beauty of Venetian buildings, from the damp course upwards, to the most exquisite polished marbles, is $CaCO_3$ in one form or another. So when it rains, the grandeur of Venice gradually fizzes away and, although you can't hear it, the evidence is all around you in those rough, pitted surfaces on which microscopic plants and algae soon begin to grow. That's why both Neptune and Zeus are crying green tears.

To add insult to injury, those thousands of pigeons that are protected, and indeed fed by the state twice a day, and gorged between meals by all those picture clicking visitors, are knocking hell out of the buildings. All those amorous coo-cooings are punctuated by the scrape of equally amorous claws against the facade, a real case of 'a lot of what the pigeons fancy does the buildings absolutely no good at all'.

Mind you, you really can't blame the pigeons, especially when you see what some of us humans do to all the treasures they reputedly come to see, well at least that is what the brochures say! 'MAN UNITED O.K.' does absolutely nothing for the left buttock of the third bronze horse of the Basilica, and surely it wasn't the real Rose Macaulay who wrote her name in red way up there on the brickwork.

For a long time the daily droppings of guano was blamed for the state of surface decay, so they cleaned it all off, exposing the stone to the ravages of feet and dilute sulphuric acid which only made things worse. So they invented artificial guano and painted it on as extra protection, the trouble was that they got the formula wrong and the oily base sank into the soft stone.

So now the pigeons are allowed to do as they have done ever since they first were granted protection by the state, to commemorate the fact that a pigeon brought back the good news of the sacking of Constantinople, way back – well it's so long ago that even the pigeons have forgotten.

My second port of call is always Chioggia, where you can see the fruits of the sea at first hand in the fish market. Mountains of glutinous squid, a surfeit of scallop shells – enough to decorate every gallon of petrol ever sold through the pumps of the world! The polished shells of Venus and millions upon millions of mussels. No, the mussels don't come from the canals, but from the modern mussel farms that punctuate the cleaner parts of the lagoon with ordered rows of piles, from which are hung the open mesh socks of polypropylene in which the mussels grow with surprising rapidity. The method is known as suspension culture and in this way the farmers can make complete use of the whole of the water column, and all those suspension feeders, themselves suspended in the flow of the tides, could not be better fed. The whole process, though labour intensive, is very productive and the products that make part of those fantastic meals are carefully checked for absolute purity at the modern fisheries' laboratory near Chioggia.

Both the port and the mussel farms are well worth a day in any tourist's itinerary, and it allows you a glimpse, at least in longshot, of the character of the lagoon before man came muscling in on the scene. This is the Venice that few visitors ever see, a world of productive muddy water, where the nadir of every view is a shimmering haze of sea and sky where time and tide meet in the mirage that is Doge City.

Fig 66 *Fish farming in the Doge's Valley*

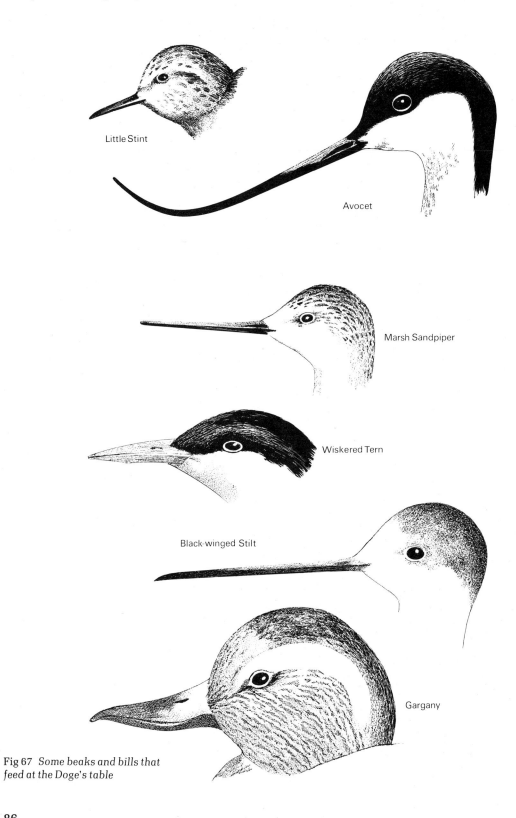

Little Stint

Avocet

Marsh Sandpiper

Wiskered Tern

Black-winged Stilt

Gargany

Fig 67 *Some beaks and bills that feed at the Doge's table*

Next time, why not shun the heat of Venice in the summer and make your visit in the cool of spring, when the lagoon itself is full of its own flocks of visitors, the migrant birds which drop in to feed in its rich waters. Golden Plover, Spotted Redshank, Greenshank, Sandpipers both Spotted and Broad Billed, Little Stint, Temmniks Stint, more than 4,000 Garganeys and a host of other birds. Or even in the winter, for then the waters are crowded with other visitors, Widgeon, Pintail, Teal, Pochard and Tufted Duck, to mention but just a few. Yes there, outside the crumbling walls of the tourist hot spot of the world, are 140,000 acres of shallow water, a paradise waiting to be explored – and it's all cheaper out of season!

Fig 68 *Istrian stone, bored by Piddocks in a past age of oxygenated water*

To top the bill, spring, summer, autumn or winter, turn right, not left, out of Marco Polo's airport: yes, turn away from Doge City and head for the Valley of the Doge, a naturalists' paradise, its clear waters alive with birds and fish. It is here, where the waters of the lagoon are fed by the silt-rich water of the River Sile, that fish farming has been practised for over 2,000 years:– and today the farms provide the bulk of the mullet and bass which find their way onto the menus of the restaurants of Venice and its environs.

This is, to me, the real magic of the Venetian scene. Great rustling banks of Reed separate the crystal clear waters and provide the wildfowl with both food and shelter. It is a tranquil place, spoilt only by the crash of guns, for it is today a wildfowl reserve, as it was when given to the Doge by the Emperor of Austria. It may seem somewhat ironical that this is the last true natural reserve of the lagoon and yet its existence depends on the slaughter of birds. Much as we may decry the 'sport' of wildfowling, there is no getting away from the fact that the wildfowlers look after their own preserves, to the benefit of at least some of the visiting birds. I will say no more, for this is a place to explore on your own, a place as remote from St Mark's Square as anywhere on earth. Yet it is always there, shimmering in stately reality, a man-made mirage, way back across the lagoon.

Hanging gardens of Atlantis

Stretching south into the azure of the Aegean is a scatter of islands, best called the Cyclades, all that remains today of an arc of land that once connected Greece and Turkey. The largest single piece of this intercontinental land bridge is the island of Crete, which has the distinction of being the most southerly part of Europe. Crete basks in the true heat of the Mediterranean climate, its southernmost shore dipping down below latitude 35°N. – and that's south of the Mason-Dixon line!

Crete is a place to visit in the green of spring, when the people of Lasithi plain begin to fit their windpumps with the sails of summer so that they can draw on the energy of the hot dry winds to lift water from the reservoirs deep in the Limestone bedrock, to irrigate their crops.

Rain falls mainly in the winter months, and the spring brings with it a crop of wild flowers enough to rival even the best of British gardens, so this is the best time to make a botanical pilgrimage. However, as Crete rises in a series of spectacular steps up to the height of mount Idi, which peaks at 2148 metres and bears a tatty cloak of summer snow; it is possible, with a little bit of travelling and some not too strenuous walking, to enjoy the spring over a full three months, stretched out by the range of altitude. In the same way, it is possible, in the span of a short stay, to experience the full spectrum of the growing season, autumn, winter, spring and aestivation.

If you want to get the full treatment, I suggest that you start at the embayment of Vai on the north-east coast, where the beach is fringed with date palms – and remember you are still in Europe. If you are saying "So what, I have seen date palms on the 'Costa Brava'", so have I, planted and nurtured in formal gardens. The date palms at Vai are not only of natural occurrence, but they are also of a type unique to Crete, *Phoenix dactylifera*; the sweet, ever-so-fattening date, *forma theophrasti*, named after the Greek naturalist, Theophrastus and found in the wild state only in Crete.

Palms are widespread throughout the tropics and a number are planted for ornament in the more temperate parts of Europe. Only the dwarf Fan Palm, which can even be grown in the warmer parts of Britain, is said to be a true native of Europe. There is even some doubt about the Cretan date as to whether

Fig 69 *Alternative technology before its time*

Fig 70 *A date with Theophrastus*

it got to Crete under its own steam, or whether it was planted way back in antiquity and has, in isolation, changed sufficiently in character to warrant the distinction of *forma* and the name of Theophrastus. Whatever its origin, its presence is enough to bring the true tang of the tropics to this corner of Europe and I reckon that, paddling in the sea at Vai one can be said to be on the international date line, phytogeographically speaking that is. To add to the feeling of tropicallity, one can also have the pleasure of visiting Europe's only commercial banana plantations which may be found nearby.

From this tropical fringe, the journey takes you in and up across dry slopes covered, as they should be in the Mediterranean climate with Maquis and Garrigue. Maquis is perhaps the most characteristic type of vegetation to be found in the Mediterranean. It consists of dense thickets of tall shrubs, many of which top two metres. The shrubs themselves suffer from twigginess, which makes the thickets painful to push one's way through, and all of them have small tough leaves. Conspicuous, especially when in flower, are the Brooms, all yellow and glorious in spring, and the great smoky masses of tiny white flowers belonging to the Tree Heather, *Erica arborea.*

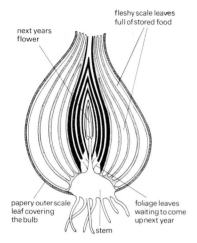

next years flower

fleshy scale leaves full of stored food

papery outer scale leaf covering the bulb

foliage leaves waiting to come up next year

stem

A BULB — *a modified bud*

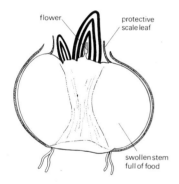

flower

protective scale leaf

swollen stem full of food

A CORM — *an underground swollen stem with a bud(s) on the top*

Fig 71 *A bulb is an underground bud. A corm is an underground stem. Check out the differences*

Garrigue is equally typical of the same climate, but grows in drier poorer situations than the Maquis. As if to demonstrate the poverty of its habitat, the shrubs are rarely more than 50 centimetres tall, their leaves much reduced, often spiny and aromatic. In Crete and indeed throughout Greece, the local name for Garrigue is 'Phrygana'. Both these types of vegetation are thus dominated by their own mixtures of evergreen shrubs, both are armed with spines, prickles and thorns, and each have a very typical understorey of geophytes, which only make their presence known in spring and autumn.

Geophytes are plants which spend the driest and/or coldest part of each year underground in the form of bulbs, corms, rhizomes or some such subterranean organ of perennation. Just as many of our plants overwinter, those of Crete oversummer (although the correct word is 'Aestivate'), safe underground, during the bad times of each year. As soon as the rains come, they can take immediate advantage of the fact and get sprouting, using up the rich reserves of food from their underground stores.

Conspicuous among these spring plants are a staggering array of Orchids, each flaunting its jewel-like flower at the hosts of insects which incessantly buzz in the heat of the spring days. It is almost an insult to select a favourite from amongst these perfect blooms; I will, however, transgress by saying that among my favourites are the Bee Orchids. The reason for my choice is not only because of their perfect beauty, nor their dumpy resemblance to the body of an insect, but mainly because of their enormous variety of form, colour and markings. Almost every one you see is slightly different, and it can be great fun to attempt to fit your particular find into one of the packets of convenience created by the ordered minds of the taxonomists. Is it a Bumble Bee, a Yellow Bee, Mirror, Woodcock, Fly, Early Spider or Late Spider? Sometimes it's easy, often it is very difficult to tell.

The best thing is to lie down with the book, especially if it's one of those super ones with coloured pictures and classify away to your heart's content! Better still, take a close up photograph, always using the same type of film to ensure that the colours are comparable, and file them away for the long winter evenings, when you can sit back at your leisure and endeavour to sort them out.

The resemblance of the flowers to the insects is not wholly fortuitous, for there is much evidence to show that the insects may be fooled into visiting the flowers for purposes other than collecting nectar or admiring their beauty. The insects may indeed think that the flower is another insect of similar ilk and, therefore, attempt to mate with it. Such acts are called 'pseudo-copulation' and, apart from boosting the insect's ego, they do effect the process of pollination, transferring the special pollen sacks from one flower to another, thus helping to maintain the continuity of the special species of Orchid.

The fact that it is often very difficult to place a single individual plant into its exact taxonomic position says little for the efficacy of pseudocopulation or for the eyesight of the lovelorn insect! To quote the flora, 'the fact is that hybridisation between the Bee Orchids is not infrequent, especially in the Mediterranean'.

If you do manage to tear your camera away from the lowland orchids even greater delights await you at a $\frac{1}{125}$th at 1200 — that is, of course, 1200 metres above sea level.

The plain of Omalos in April is a Cretan must; the edge of its haphazard fields overflow with a riot of Anemones and little pink tulips, an ideal place to sit down, drink in the view and sort out your basic botany.

The flowering plants may be conveniently divided into two basic groups, the Monocotyledons and the Dicotyledons, the main feature of distinction being the number of seed leaves (Cotyledons) found in the seed and usually on the very young plant. There are, however, a number of other very constant features which serve to distinguish between members of these two groups and these are listed in the table below. The delicate Pink Tulip is a Monocotyledon, while the anemones are typical of the second great class of plants.

MONOCOTYLEDONS AND DICOTYLEDONS CHECK THEIR FEATURES

Dicotyledons	Monocotyledons
Embryo with two seed leaves (Cotyledons)	Embryo with one seed leaf (Cotyledon)
Leaves simple or compound	Leaves always simple
Leaves usually net veined, that means that the veins branch from the midrib and the branches, divide again and again	Leaves usually parallel veined, that is all the veins run parallel to each other
Primary (main) root usually present throughout the life of the plant	Primary root is usually replaced by many smaller adventitious roots growing from the base of the stem
Flowers often with distinct sepals and petals	Flowers never with distinct sepals and petals

Next, savour the beauty of the anemones and get ready for a pleasant surprise, because they are very closely related to our ever-so-common yellow buttercups, all being members of the same family, the *Ranunculaceae*. Each has the family characteristics of separate showy petals surrounding a great mass of anthers which are seated on the head of the flower stalk in an ever decreasing, or increasing spiral, depending from which end you start. The spiral arrangement of the parts of the flower is said to be a primitive characteristic and the Buttercup family is reckoned to have developed early in the evolution of the flowering plants. Anemones may be members of the Buttercup family, but they are not buttercups, a fact that can easily be checked, lift up the petals and take a look. All true buttercups (genus *Ranunculus*) have a number of sepals, the job of which was to protect the flower while in bud: the true anemones (genus *Anemone*) lack sepals, the protective role being taken over by modified leaves called bracts. Even if you never get to Crete, check out the difference on home grown Wood Anemones (*Anemone nemorosa*).

Crete is, however, one of the places where it is very easy to come to the wrong conclusion because here, one true buttercup comes in all shades from buttercup yellow, through scarlet to pure white. The plant is question is *Ranunculus asiaticus*, however, a quick look under the showy petals will be proof enough that everyone can tell the difference between anemones and buttercups. Another point distinguishing these two Cretan relatives, at least in Crete, is that the Buttercup is never found growing as high up as the Anemone.

This fact gives us a clue as to why both the Cretan Anemone and the, not so delicate, Pink Tulip (*Tulipa bakeri*) may be found in the seedsman's catalogues and be grown in English gardens. At 1,200 metres, even in this the most southerly part of Europe, the climate is not all that different from that we left back home when we came to take our rare dose of spring sunshine in all its glory. However, to see these Cretan plants in all *their* glory there is only one place, high on the Omalos plain with a backdrop of the snowy White Mountains.

In among all the Latin names which crowd the slopes of a Cretan spring, the name of the island appears again and again in the specific epithet – Cretica, which simply means 'of Crete'. In many cases the name means just that, of Crete and only of Crete, the proper word for such a plant whose distribution is limited to one country is 'endemic'.

Some 138 of Crete's glorious flowering plants are said to be endemic and the reason becomes more and more obvious as one climbs up onto the heights of the mountains. White they are

Fig 72 Some plants of Crete
(a) *Ebenus cretica*
(b) *Alyssoides cretica*
(c) *Ranunculus asiaticus*
(d) *Iris cretica*
(e) *Anemone coronaria*

called and white they are, and even the hardy British traveller will be glad of the tour operator's instructions – 'You are advised to bring a thick sweater'! At 1,800 metres above sea level there is a truly montane climate and the upper slopes are picked out with real montane flowers which grow in splendid isolation from their nearest montane neighbours.

Large as the Cretan mainland may be, it is still an island and it is separated from all other land masses. In like manner her mountains are, in fact, islands within the island, each one an oasis for montane plants set within a sea of hot dry lowlands, themselves set in a sea of sea. So it has been for a very long time and so, in isolation from all other populations of montane plants, the Cretan populations have gone their own sweet evolutionary way, producing new species in their eyries of endemism. It is not only the montane plants, the flora of many of the other vegetation types also share a high degree of endemism.

Favourite among the Cretan endemics is the White Cyclamen, which is found throughout the island and is a fitting tribute to the process of evolution in isolation.

There is, however, one much more widespread plant that can help our understanding of the processes by which evolution spawns new species. *Nigella arvensis*, Love in the Mist is a common plant throughout Greece, Crete and the islands of the Cretan Sea down into the mainland of Turkey. Detailed study of this widespread plant has shown that it is very variable and comes in a great variety of sizes and forms; and no less than ten recognisable species and subspecies have been described from the area. *Nigella arvensis* ssp *arvensis* is found in northern Greece, while *Nigella doefleri* is found in Crete, the latter being so different from the former that it has been separated off as another species, which it is not, at least in strict botanical terms. Distinct species, at least by one set of definitions, are incompatible with each other, which means that they cannot interbreed. The two types of Love in the Mist in question never do interbreed because their populations are separated one from the other. However, if they are brought together, pollination is possible and some hybrid seed will be set. In their natural state of geographical isolation, each is going its own sweet love-in-the-mist way towards becoming a separate species which will be both geographically and genetically isolated.

For us human beings who can jet about the world, geographical isolation may appear and probably is unimportant; and certainly, in his travels, man has carried seeds with him, thus breaking down millions of years of geographical isolation.

However, under natural conditions such isolation is important and may, indeed, be a prime mover in the process of speciation – and the top of the White Mountain is an ideal place to remember just how big the world is in non jet set terms. It is also a good place to sit and see that same jet age catching up with an island that has its roots almost as deep in the history of civilisation as any other. The traditional goats are there eating their way through the beauty of spring, but new mechanical aids are deep ploughing up the underground parts of the geophytes and leaving them to die in the heat of the sun. Worse still booms spray-out selective herbicides which, though ideal for the farmer, are spelling doom to the cacaphony of beautiful flowers which attract so many of the island's visitors. There are still as many places where the fallow fields are as much an attraction for the tourist as is the rich bouquet of produce, grown in those same fields when under crop. Annual Chrysanthemums, some varieties being as big and blooming as any we grow in our gardens, blaze their colour across the island and, in places they form a brilliant background for the pink spikes of the little Gladiolus. But for how much longer? No, do not judge the Cretan farmers too harshly, we have already done the same, destroying the beauty of our fallow fields in the cause of higher productivity.

It seems likely that only in the remoteness of the mountain tops and on the steep cliffs, which give many parts of Crete a very rugged character, will the Cretan flora, with its more than

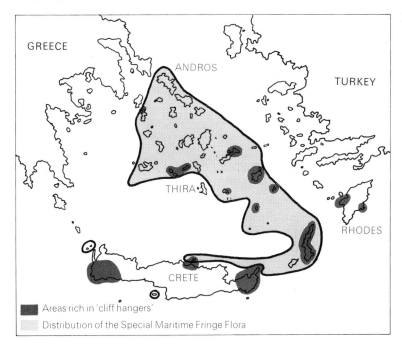

Fig 73 *The remnants of Atlantis and its Flora?*

GREECE

ANDROS

TURKEY

THIRA

RHODES

CRETE

■ Areas rich in 'cliff hangers'

Distribution of the Special Maritime Fringe Flora

usual number of endemics, survive the onslaught of these modern 'crimes'. At the least, they will be forced to exist in smaller and smaller areas, refugia, where they may be wiped out or further evolution may in time confirm upon them the distinction of rarity through new endemism.

Apart from the array of endemics, the plants which live on the cliffs have some other very interesting characteristics. First, the botanists have given them the nice collective name of Chasmophytes, the plants which live in crevices often hanging off the edge of a chasm. Secondly, they often grow in glorious isolation each from the next and rarely come into direct competition with a next door neighbour. In fact, the only time that competition raises its ugly head amongst the cliff hangers is when their seeds are about to become established. Most of the seeds will fall on solid rock with never a nook or cranny to tempt a blue blooded Chasmophyte. Only a very few will get into a suitable crevice and, in most cases, these will already be full to overflowing with other hangers on, so regeneration is a real dead man's crevice situation.

The Chasmophyte has only one escape route and that is upwards, because downwards, the route is terminated by more gently sloping rocks, which will be clothed in a more stable vegetation, lots of competition and no place for a Chasmophyte. Up it must be and there's the problem which has been solved by the majority of the cliff dwellers having very light seeds that will be carried by the up-currents of air to higher points on the cliff face. Another way of keeping up with the Chasmophytes is ladder scrambling, the leader shoot of the plant growing upwards to find root space one step above. It is possible to see this at work on our own brick walls where Chasmophytes, like the Ivy Leaved Toadflax, ladder their way up. Unfortunately, in nature the root holds are irregularly placed and often a long way apart, making this type of ascent impossible.

There are some Chasmophytes whose seeds are supplied with oil bodies to attract ants, who come and carry the seed away. Ants are good climbers and certainly could thus provide for short distance transport, the ants themselves storing the seeds in crevices in which they may germinate. The insects really come into their own when it comes to pollination of the Chasmophytes, most of these having showy and/or scented flowers, ideal for attracting their airborne pollinators.

So it is that the community of cliff hangers live out their chosen precarious existence, an existence which, though it appears to teeter on the brink of disaster, cannot be all that bad for the plants concerned. On the good side, they are subject to little or no competition, zero grazing by larger animals; and

Opposite page
Some Orchids of Crete

(Chapter Seven)

Top left
Ophrys fuciflora

Top right
Ophrys cretica

Middle left
Ophrys apifera

Middle centre
Ophrys tenthredinifera

Middle right
Ophrys sphegodes

Bottom left
Ophrys scolopax

Bottom right
Ophrys muscifera

they are safe from the process of succession, which would in time turn a less vertical habitat into more closed vegetation – phrygara or even garrigue. The only tree which inserts itself into the cliff-hanging act is the funeral cypress, *Cupressus sempervirens*, sub-species *horizontalis* and, as it can only grow in the largest cracks, it never really challenges the openness of the cliff habitat. So it is that the chasmophyte communities probably represent vegetation types of very long standing in which, if you have the ability to sit tight, often to make do with very little water, then you can hang about for a very long time, isolated on the rocks.

It may provide at least some measure of comfort and perhaps even hope to speculate on the fact that this is not the first time when the flora of this area has been forced to retreat.

Fig 74 *It would have been nice to be King of the Minoans (Throne room at Knossos)*

Back in the Bronze Age, there was a culture which held its sway from Crete clear across the Cyclades to the mainland of Greece. The name was the Minoan and the Minoans were traders, their whole wealth and influence depending upon their coastal towns, ports and sea routes. One island called Thera, situated some 50 km north of Crete, although part of their domain, was to be the source of their destruction. Thera is a gigantic volcano and, in the winter of 1470 BC, it blew its top in a cataclysm that must have ranked alongside the much more infamous Krakatoa.

Great tidal waves, created by an enormous volume of rock falling into the sea, rushed out from Thera destroying everything in their path, including all the main settlements of the Minoans, and those who were not killed by the first onrush of water were doomed to die in other ways.

Opposite page

The old forest Bieloweja

(Chapter Eight)

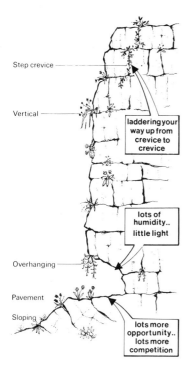

Step crevice

Vertical

laddering your
way up from
crevice to
crevice

lots of
humidity..
little light

Overhanging

Pavement

Sloping

lots more
opportunity..
lots more
competition

Fig 75 *Habitats for hangers-on*

One can only imagine the terror created by the series of tidal waves, followed by a blanket of volcanic dust or tephra which fell covering an area of 300,000 sq km, a choking blanket of death. To understand the magnitude of the cataclysm, you must go to Thera and view all that remains of the once gigantic volcano and the pitiful remnants of a Minoan town protruding from the base of a cliff of pumice over 35 metres high. Only modern deep sea drilling has revealed the true extent of the deposit of tephra which gets thinner and thinner with increasing distance from the epicentre of the explosion. The surmise that the explosion occurred in winter is based on the pattern of deposition of the tephra, for it is downwind of the island in the direction of the winds of the winter period. Crete did not escape and was, in part, covered with a deposit of a mere 10 cm of dust. However, from the Krakatoa experience, it is known that 10 cm is sufficient to smother the crops and much of the natural vegetation of an area. So the surviving Minoans, their main nexus of trade smashed, were doomed to starvation.

Likewise much of the natural flora was smothered, the only places escaping such destruction were the hanging gardens of the cliff faces where the tephra could not collect. Today it is to these cliffs that many of the botanists claw their way to pay their homage to the stalwart flora of Crete for, like the mountain tops, these habitats harbour many endemics which enjoy both restricted and disjunct distribution.

It is not difficult to imagine the scene of desolation. The tephra would only slowly have disappeared, weathered away by time and climate, eventually to form new productive soil. It may well have cleared first from the lowest lying zones, where it could be washed away by wave action during bad weather, thus opening up the areas for colonisation.

Just as the Minoan culture has been the subject of detailed study in the past few years, so too has the flora of the islands of the Cretan Sea, in fact a group of Scandinavian botanists have made it their pleasant task to visit all the islands of the archipelago. Their work has shown that the diversity of vegetation present is related to the size of the island in question; the bulk of the islands, however being covered with phyrgana. The lowest sectors of each island are, of course, washed by salt water, especially during bad weather, and they support a vegetation dominated by salt tolerant plants, the majority of which are of common occurrence throughout the Mediterranean. There is often a zone of great floristic interest found between the salt marshes and the phrygana proper, a zone best called maritime. Although it is a very poor type of vegetation to look at, it is very rich in rare species.

On the smallest of the islands there is no phrygana and their total vegetation falls into the category of 'maritime fringe'. The really fascinating thing is, that of the few plants which typify this maritime vegetation, nine are only found on these small islands, thirteen more are mainly confined to such islands and no less than ten are endemic to the islands of the Aegean. Add to this the fact that the distribution of these plants appears to be very haphazard, there is no basic explicable pattern in their distribution, which all adds up to a highly peculiar state of affairs.

Everything points to the fact that what we see today is a mere disjunct remnant, all that remains of what was once a much more widespread flora, a flora with some pretty unique characteristic plants of its own.

The facts all begin to fit, we know that a million years ago the land bridge was in place. It was a vast area and could well have supported its own natural life styles. As the sea level rose, the land bridge gradually broke up into the scatter of islands, leaving many of the populations of plants stranded, isolated on their way to endemism.

A great mass of land now hidden under the azure waves, a land mass with a character of its own, a great civilisation lost to a cataclysm and buried in tephra; could this have been Atlantis and would it be too much to look upon the cliff and 'maritime fringe' vegetation of the cyclades as the hanging gardens of that lost civilisation?

No-man's-land

Evolution must have started somewhere! Wherever you like to begin your deliberations, be it the first 'bag' of living chemicals floating in the primeval, till then, lifeless firmament; or the moment when Adam first found himself in the Garden of Eden, the same is true. At some point on the earth, and at some exact point of time in prehistory, each and every plant and animal must have had its origin. Take for example the Common Dandelion. At some time in the past there was no plant which could have borne the name *Taraxacum officinale*. There must have been many plants very like it, but evolution had not yet proceeded far enough to produce a population of plants that were distinct enough from all other members of the tribe *Cichoriaceae* in the great family of the Compositae to bear the name of *Taraxacum*. At some time and place the first definitive *Taraxacum officinale* must have raised its plate of golden-yellow flowers and produced its 'clock' of silken parachutes – its time had come! From that moment on the world had a new flower and, from that point in space they began to spread out to colonise much of the northern hemisphere.

At the bottom of each of the silken parachutes is a small fruit called an Achene, inside each fruit is a single seed and each seed contains all the genetic information needed to make a new Dandelion. The fascinating thing is that in 99·999 plus cases out of 100 the new dandelion will look just like its parent because dandelions are Apomicts. Apomicts are plants which have the ability to produce seeds directly from the ovules, without pollination and fertilisation having taken place. No fertilisation means that the offspring will have exactly the same genetic makeup as its single parent and hence should look exactly the same.

Next time you mow the lawn or collect leaves for your pet rabbit, or have half an hour to spare while on holiday, take a real close look at the local dandelions. You will discover that there is an enormous range of variation between the different plants: large leaves, small leaves, leaves which are deeply cut into fine segments and those which are almost entire. Tall flowers, short flowers and so it goes on, the members of each sub-population are true to the characteristics of their parent yet there is no getting away from the fact that they all are Dandelions.

Over the years of Dandelion evolution there has, however, been a certain amount of genetic change and mixing, so much

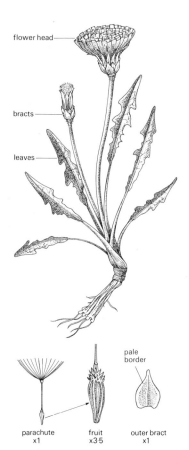

Fig 76 *A Dandelion, a successful design for life in damp places*

flower head

bracts

leaves

parachute
x1

fruit
x3·5

pale
border

outer bract
x1

TARAXACUM OFFICINALE L. *SECTION PALUSTRIA*

so that a number of more or less distinct lines have evolved and the interesting thing is that the most distinct of these lines are each confined to specific habitats, where they continue to show off their more unique features.

So it is that, today, we can find dandelions throughout the northern hemisphere. From the tops of mountains down to the coastline, the Genus *Taraxacum* is doing well and evolution is going on, fitting certain lines of the Dandelion clan to certain habitats. The main types of Dandelion to be found in Britain are listed in the table below, together with their key features and chosen habitats. Try it for yourself, can you tell the difference between one lot of Dandelions and the next?

HOW TO KNOW YOUR DANDELIONS

The genus Taraxacum includes about 2,000 species. The British Dandelions are best looked upon, not as separate species but as Tribes of variation within the species *Taraxacum officinale*. There are five such tribes which with a bit of patience and perserverence you should be able to recognise. Here are the details prepared for our edification by Dr John Richards, one of the kings of Taraxacum Taxonomy.

Name of 'Tribe' or section	Size of Plant	Leaves	Outer Bracts of flower head	Fruits	Habitat
vulgaria	Large	Some with dark blotches between leaf lobes No spots	Erect to recurved	Straw coloured to brown (3·5 mm)	Disturbed Places Weeds
spectabilia	Medium to large	Many black spots often with red purple leaf stalks and midribs	Spreading to adpressed	Straw to brown (3·5-5·5 mm)	Wet climates, heaths, grassland meadows, rarely a weed
palustria	Small to medium	Linear, smooth, few lobes. No markings	Adpressed ovate with pale or thin paper like border	Brown (3·0-4·5 mm)	Wet base rich fens, where winter flooding occurs, never a weed
erythrosperma	Small, delicate	No markings. Leaf very cut up into narrow segments	Lance shaped, erect to recurved usually with a small tooth-like projection just below apex	Violet, purple, Red-cinnamon, or brown (less than 3·5 mm)	Likes warm places, heaths, dunes, sometimes walls, rarely weeds
obliqua	Small	Narrow leaves with many lobes	As above	As above	Dune, grassland and slacks

Apart from keeping all wandering botanists on their taxonomic toes, the Dandelions do help to demonstrate the importance of borders and boundaries.

Borders and boundaries are places of change and, as such, they represent a challenge to all living things. Perhaps that is why we humans often spend an inordinate amount of time endeavouring to cross them! We all, do like to be beside the seaside, which is perhaps the best border of all, and lakes and rivers come a close second when it comes to attracting humans. We have, of course, created many boundaries of our own, they range from hedgerows, through autobahns, to great political boundaries, the latter often following the course of a natural boundary line.

Many of the natural boundaries are not as clear cut as the wet/dry, sea/land type, some being very diffuse and even gradually on the move. Perhaps that is the difference, a boundary is a dividing line marking the end of one thing and the beginning of the next. A border is a zone of change between the two adjacent things. However, it must be accepted that, if a border is a recognisable entity, then it is a complex of boundaries; Thing A – boundary – border – boundary – thing B. Complicated, isn't it? Perhaps it's best just to accept the fact that borders/boundaries are places of change between two adjacent phenomena and use the term 'No Man's Land'.

Sweeping across Europe are a number of tracts of no man's land between contrasting climates and hence vegetation types. Perhaps the most important is that between the extensive coniferous forests of the Sub-Arctic, the Great Boreal Forest which encircles the northern hemisphere with an evergreen halo, and the mixed deciduous forest of the warmer, more southern climes. The border between these productive forest-scapes is very wide, in places almost 1,000 km and in it a mixture of both types of trees can be found. It is indeed so wide that the border forests are looked upon as a type in their own right and are called the Sub-Boreal Mixed Forests.

The evergreen conifers are well adapted to life in the higher latitudes where, during the long dark winter when the ground is frozen solid, their needle leaves lose very little water. When the spring comes the leaves are there in position ready to fix all the energy needed for growth and storage ready for the next winter. The deciduous trees, on the other hand, get rid of their leaves each autumn thereby overcoming the problem of winter water loss. Their main problem, however, is to store sufficient energy to tide them over the winter to get the buds bursting and the leaves unfolding ready to begin photosynthesising next spring. Thus it is that each of the types of trees are best adapted to their own climatic zone. There is no doubt that they could grow in either climatic belt, but they would be at an enormous disadvantage in competition with the local 'boss' trees, and hence the two types of forest remain more or less distinct.

In no man's land it is a different matter, both sorts can grow as well as each other. If it is a hard winter the conifers may win, whereas in a long, warm summer the broad leaved trees may be at an advantage. No man's land is, in fact, everyman's land, but in it everyman, or rather every tree lives a more precarious existence.

I have always wondered what this swathe of no man's land was like before man came onto the scene and removed much of the forest. I presume that as you progressed further north the conifers increased in importance at the expense of the others until finally you had made it up into the Taiga, land of the conifer.

Fig 77 *House and Gardens prize-winning TV aerial? No, a stork at its nest, a not uncommon sight along the Polish border*

There is, however, at least one area where you can see a small part of this borderland almost in its natural state, and there is one very special spot on which I like to stand contemplating the importance of borders. The place is Sidra, near Bialystok in eastern Poland, and the spot is at the top of a peculiar mound which rises some 10 metres above the surrounding terrain. From a distance the mound looks like a slightly elongate bell-barrow, 150 metres long by 120 metres wide, sitting in the middle of a lush, green field.

As you approach the mound the dandelions change from *T. officinale* to *T. palustre*, although you don't need a flora to discern the change as the ground gets decidedly wetter. The mound is surrounded by a wet fen in which all sorts of super plants are growing. I think my greatest surprise was to find masses of Jacobs Ladder (a plant which in England seems to favour limestone cliffs), growing with its roots well and truly in the water. The really surprising thing is, however, that the mound itself is covered with the same fen plants, Mosses, Sedges, Kingcups etc, which grow around its base, even Greater Spearwort grows in abundance on the steep sides. The mound must therefore be very wet and it is, in fact, the source of the water which nurtures the fen and flows away downslope as a sparkling clear stream. It is quite a scramble to get to the top of the mound and as you go it gets wetter and wetter. About half way up a spring gushes to the surface and, even on the very apex water oozes up around your feet. From the top it is easy to see the source of the water. The sides of the valley slope steeply up away from the fen to a height of about 30 metres above fen level. Any rain falling on and soaking into the catchment will press down on the water held in the porous rock, increasing the pressure in the ground-water system. The mound actually sits on the site of an artesian spring, whose hydrostatic pressure keeps the whole thing saturated. All you need to do to prove it is to climb to the top of the mound after heavy rain, poke a stick into the apex and water comes gushing up in a small fountain.

The mound is a Spring Mire and, although I have seen them in a number of other places, this is, to my knowledge, the largest in existence.

Although the mound owes its existence to the hydrostatic pressure of the spring, it is not in fact held up by it. If it were, a hole poked in the top would bring about immediate subsidence as the life blood of the spring mire leaked away. The mound consists of layers of peat and a special sort of limestone known as tufa. The spring water is charged with calcium bicarbonate and, when it reaches the surface it meets the roots

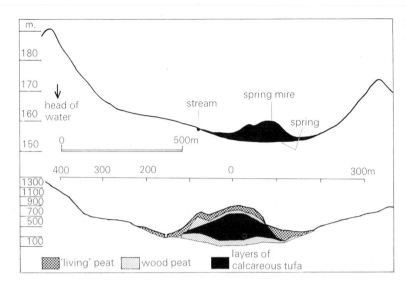

Fig 78 *The biggest spring mire of them all*

of all the plants, which produce a dilute solution of carbonic acid as a byproduct of their respiration. The two chemicals react and calcium carbonate is produced, encasing the plants with a mass of crumbly limestone (the tufa). So the process continues, layer after layer of peat and tufa are laid down and will continue to be laid down until the height of the mound is sufficient to contain the head of spring water. Then and only then, will the mound stop growing and the rich fen communities be gradually replaced by those more typical of the mixed forest. As this happens, one of the first trees to come in on the surface of the mound is, what must be the rarest of the European birches, *Betula humilis*, which looks not unlike a larger bushy version of the dwarf birch, *Betula nana*, which grows in some abundance in a few places in Scotland. *Betula humilis* is not a British plant and has a somewhat restricted distribution in Europe, making its home in boundary situations where the flow of rich fen water is being impeded and the vegetation is beginning to change from open fen to forest.

From the top of my very special mound at Sidra, I like to stand on tiptoe and look north towards the Taiga, south towards the rich deciduous forest and east towards the promised land of the Pripet Marshes. I hasten to add that this is only the promised land for people like me who spend much of their life studying peatlands. Every member of the honorary order of peatnicks has heard of the Pripet Marshes, thanks to one of the kings of the peatnicks – Stanislaw Kulczynski. As a young research worker, back in the early '30s he was given the job of surveying this enormous area of swamp and peatlands in which the rivers Bug, Vistula and Pripet have their origins.

Not only did Kulczynski accomplish this fantastic task, he laid the foundations of the modern study of vegetation by employing, for the first time, mathematical methods to help him sort his phenomenal amount of field data.

I was very privileged, as a student, to work with Kulczynski and to stand with him on top of the Spring Mire, looking out towards the Pripet Marshes, as he explained the importance of boundaries to me.

The whole area around Sidra abounds with boundaries and, of the whole of Europe, this must be one of the largest lowland areas which are but little affected by man. The Pripet Marshes are today in Soviet Russia, and the border between Poland and the largest country in the world is a no man's land in which development has, fortunately, not gone on quite as fast as it has in the landscape of the two adjoining countries. One name appears again and again on the maps of the border area, and that is Puczca, a name that means Wilderness, and they are just that, areas for which, thankfully, man has so far found no use.

The largest wilderness in the vicinity of Sidra is the Red Mire, a vast tract of fen and bog land in which it is all too easy to get lost. The only tracks which lead into this place each end in a scatter of stunted birch and, from then on in, it's a wet and, in summer a hot job to discover the secrets of the Red Mire. Close to the land rim of the fen are hummocks, small in comparison with the record Spring Mire, but certainly large as hummocks go. They come in all shapes and a staggering variety of colours, from blanched green, through black-red to a wonderful golden brown. Each one is made of a single species of Bog Moss and my favourites are the brown ones which are made of *Sphagnum fuscum*.

Bog mosses usually shun calcareous water and are usually found growing in positions where their main water and mineral supply comes from the rain falling directly on top of them. As they grow, they produce acidic wastes which gradually acidify the habitat in which they are growing. The *Sphagnum* hummocks along the edge of the Red Mire are growing in highly calcareous water and the proof is there – squelching in all their glory are the same plants which grow on the top of the great Spring Mire of Sidra. Each bog moss hummock sits there, pouring out its wastes, an acid island in a sea of flowing calcareous water. Just think of all the mini boundaries and borders around the base of each hummock, each one an abrupt change between acid and alkaline conditions. There is no need just to think about them, they are there, each one picked out by the golden yellow of a moss called *Camptothecium nitens*, a

THE BORDERERS

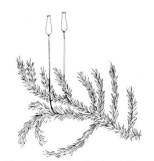

Fig 79 *Camptothecium nitens*
(*A golden moss*)

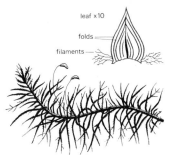

leaf x10

folds

filaments

Fig 80 *Helodium blandovii*
(*Once grew in England*)

Fig 81 *Carex chordorrhiza* (*One of the rarest plants of Scotland*)

plant which is, without doubt, the best of the borderers. It is in such places that this moss finds its own particular home, around the hummocks of these mixed mire communities.

Camptothecium nitens is only a start for, the further one proceeds into the Red Mire, more and more boundaries come into evidence, each picked out by its own special plants.

It is tough going, pushing your way through the primaeval vegetation. In places there are tracks where duck boarding has been laid in the past to make the going a little easier. The only problem is that these board tracks don't go very far, much of their structure is already crumbling away and where there is any left high and dry, it is, more often than not, already occupied. No – not by another struggling botanist but by a handsome specimen of the European Viper or Adder, which can grow to a length well in excess of 60 cm. They are not all that easy to see for even their diamond pattern blends well into the mottled background of lichen and decaying wood. A bite from a big one can spell real trouble even for the largest, healthiest botanist. So my advice is, steer clear of the tracks, stick to the rough going and keep your eyes open! The latter doesn't seem so bad if you remember that snakes cannot close their eyes because they do not have eyelids.

However careful you are I would guarantee that you will get bitten while you are on the Red Mire, not by the adders but by *Tabanus sudeticus*, the Elk Fly. Adders, fortunately, come in ones and rarely in twos, even on the Red Mire; Elk Flies come in droves, the only advantage is that you can hear them coming. In they come, homing onto that succulent, sweaty smell that is You. Mzzz and, just like the doodlebugs of World War II, it's OK so long as you can hear them buzzing, once their engines stop it could be your turn! There is, however, still time for you to take evasive action because the Elk Fly is a fussy feeder and, once settled, it has a good old clart about before getting its proboscis dug in. Once it has chosen its spot the painful bit is

Fig 82 *Betula humilis*
(*The little Birch*)

over very quickly, although the end result is a nasty hard lump which can last for a day. Once the proboscis has been dug in, it is a debateable point exactly what to do, let it feed and fly away satisfied or clout it and get a rapid injection of your own blood back plus anything else it had in its digestive system. If you are a fanatical conservationist, you might just cherish the thought of having an Elk as a blood brother. The most expedient thing to do is get it while it is still at the clarting about stage. I well remember my first encounter with *Tabanus sudeticus*, it was in southern Germany where, in the absence of Elk they are called Deer Fly. I was standing in one of my favourite peat bogs with David Streeter, of Nature Parliament fame, and the moment of decision had come. A Deer Fly had settled on my back and David Streeter took evasive action on my behalf with his anorak. I ended up on the ground with a bad dose of stove-in-ribs, the fly got up, bit me and flew off. So be careful when on the Red Mire, Elk Flies are a-coming and anti-histamines are in sight, so my advice is – keep well covered and sweat it out.

Fig 83 *We can come out now the Elk Flies have gone*

The Red Mire is well worth the sweat because wherever there are Elk Flies there should be Elk, and there are. I presume that their thick, shaggy coats which are built for the long winter provide them with some measure of fly protection. However, watching them in the summer I often wondered whether they suffer from the heat, until I found out that they are not only good swimmers, but that they can actually stay completely submerged for more than sixty seconds, thus cooling and de-flying themselves both at the same time.

In summer the Elks lead a more or less solitary existence, the cows only enjoying the company of their young. However, at the onset of winter, they congregate into herds led by a female with young. The European Elk is one of the recent success stories in nature conservation, these eminently huntable animals which have been hounded to extinction in many parts of Europe, the herds of the Red Mire and its environs are now under State protection and on the increase.

In amongst the wet vastness of the mire there are a number of small clay islands, patches of drier diversity bearing areas of mixed forest within the continuum of swamp and fenland. Each island has its own complex of boundaries and each border has its own special vegetation. Passing towards one of these islands, both the terrain and the vegetation change as if the forest is reaching out to colonise the mire and the mire is reaching inwards to drown the forest. In amongst the mixture of Alder and Birch, there are two plants which appear to have made their main habitat in this dynamic border situation. The first is a sedge called *Carex chordorrhiza*, its tall flowering stems arising singly from an isolated tuft of leaves. If you look carefully you will find that, radiating out from the single tuft are long, underground rhizomes, each bearing another plant at its end, the whole population of individual plants being beautifully spaced out through the community. *Carex chordorrhiza* is a member of the group of sedges which have only one type of flowering spike, which forms a more or less lobed head on the top of the stem. The second plant is much more insignificant, a light green moss with a regularly pinnate (feather like) branch pattern, its name *Helodium blandovii*. Although of common occurrence in the colder parts of both Europe and North America, in the warmer parts of these land masses it appears restricted to boundary situations. There is some evidence to suggest that, at some time in the past, both these plants have been of more widespread occurrence and, with the warming of the climate in recent times, they have retreated to these boundary refugia. It is of interest that in Britain both species are found only in one or two localities, the former in a very restricted area of Sutherland in Scotland, the latter in three mires in England, although it may well today be extinct in our country.

What is the reason for these special boundary plants? Could it be that, in these betwixt and between spots, neither of the two adjacent plant communities can exert their presence to the full and so there is room for other plants, which are perhaps less able to tolerate competition, to survive? The answer is that we don't know. There is, however, no getting away from

Fig 84 *Decay and new growth, the age-old cycle of Bieloweja*

the fact that such boundaries are dangerous places in which to attempt to survive. If the drainage pattern of the area changes or is changed in any way, the first thing to be altered will be the boundaries. The problem is that, if the boundary shifts too quickly, the small populations of its special plants may not be able to 'shift' rapidly enough to accommodate to the change. It isn't nearly so bad for the plants of the adjacent communities, for the simple reason that their populations are much larger and it would take a much greater change to destroy their much more extensive habitats.

South of the Red Mire complex the forestscapes change, the mixture of conifers giving way to the full glory of deciduous forest.

There is still a great tract of the primaeval forest that has remained in a more or less semi-natural state. It is the Urwald (Old Forest) of Bialowieza, which spans the border between Russia and Poland, hiding the fact under a diverse mantle of fourteen different species of tree. Hornbeam, Oak, Lime, Ash, Alder, Maple, Aspen, two Birches, two Elms and Wild Apple make up the deciduous complement, while Pine and Spruce add the final touch of the conifers. The absence of Beech from the list may seem strange, but Bialowieza is beyond its northern limit in central Europe. Long, cold winters is the 'trademark' of the continental climate and Beech evidently does not like this aspect of the continental winters.

The total area of the Great Forest is 485 sq miles and within its confines are a whole range of forest communities. On the better soil of the southern half of the area the forest is dominated by a mixture of Oak and Hornbeam, Remote Flowered Sedge, *Carex remota*, and the Great Fescue, *Festuca gigantea*, both of which are common in our English woodlands are conspicuous members of the ground flora wherever the ground water table comes near to the surface. On the more freely draining soils, the Hairy Sedge, *Carex pilosa*, and the spring flowering blue *Anemone hepatica* take over as the characteristic plants.

In contrast, the more northerly part of the area bears a mixture of Oak, Birch, Poplar, Spruce and Pine. Here the soils are poorer in nutrients and are more acid, and Bilberry often makes its appearance as a member of the ground flora. So it is that even within this, the most primaeval forest remnant in Europe, there are still a mixture of communities and boundaries between them. Is this the natural pattern, or has it been 'forced' on the forest by past management and sylviculture? We may never know, but at least work is going on in an attempt to find out. Polish botanists are studying the makeup of the pollen which falls to the ground, both within and around the Urwald

each year. The modern pollen spectra can then be compared with the sub-fossil pollen spectra obtained from the peat deposits, both within the present forest and in other areas of Poland. It is tedious and painstaking work and it will be a long time before they are sure as to the actual effects of man on the forest area.

Whether natural or not, a walk through the Bialowieza forest is a never-to-be-forgotten experience and I always feel that it is the nearest one can get to a Tropical Rain Forest in Europe. For a start, over much of the forest the ground flora is very sparse, the continuous tree canopy about 25 metres above your head shuts out most of the light. The Hornbeam, Maple and Elm which make up the bulk of this canopy all have tall, thin trunks and many of the types look not unlike long handled mops, their thin trunks going straight up without any branches below their ridiculously small crowns. Every now and again, amongst the scatter of slender trunks, are single individual or small groups of really massive boles which disappear un-branched through the canopy, themselves bursting into branch some 10 metres higher. Among these massive, emergent giants are some king Spruces which tower up and up to the immense height of 45 metres, well – immense at least by central European standards. To me, they are the sentinels of the forest, looking out across the boundaries, both man made and natural, kings of their forest reserve.

It has always been a desire of mine to visit Bialowieza in the winter, when the snow blanket is down and only the scattered conifers add their warm, dark greens to the landscape.

If the trees of Bialowieza are something to write home about, and they certainly are, so too are the animals which find protection, both summer and winter, within the confines of the forest. Wolves still roam the glades of winter and Wild Pig root up the acorns of summer before they have had a chance to raise their seed-leaves above the rich forest soil. The Russian Bear takes no notice of the border signs when he pays his irregular visits to the Polish side.

Way back in 1557, legislation was brought in in an attempt to regulate the hunting of Elk, Beaver and Roe Deer. Un-fortunately, the Aurochs, *Bos taurus primigenius*, went the way of all good-eating flesh and was extinct by 1627. The European Bison, *Bison bonasus*, was somewhat luckier. Once widespread throughout the Deciduous Forest zone, its popula-tions were cut back and back, both due to hunting and to destruction of its forest habitat, until, by the beginning of the last century, it was only to be found in two areas, the Bialo-wieza and in a forest in the Caucasus.

Fig 85 *Doing well now we have discovered Zubrowka Vodka*

Protected in the hunting reserve, it did well until the Napoleonic wars when its numbers were reduced to about 300 animals. Subsequently protection, which included feeding, brought about a doubling of the numbers but also made the Bison unafraid of man. So much so that they fell easy prey to the hungry solders of the first world war, and the population was reduced down to about 150, and finally in 1921 the last of the Polish Bison were shot, and the few remaining in the Caucasus were slaughtered in 1925.

Fortunately, there were some animals left in zoos and parks, and these have formed the basic stock for a remarkable story of the conservation of this very interesting animal. In 1929 two Bison were sent to Poland and, from then on, the population has never looked back, despite the Second World War there were forty-four in 1945 and today there are somewhere between 230 and 250 living free in the forest, 26 in a strict reservation and six specially kept for the tourists to see. I don't really like seeing animals in cages, but the story of the Bison is certainly a story to back up the enormously important work done in the Zoos of the world. Without those few in captivity, *Bison bonasus* would now be in memory as dead as the proverbial Dodo.

Fig 86 *Bison grass*

Whenever I go to see the magnificent six in their enclosure, (it's there simply to keep us tourists out), I always take along a bunch of the grass *Heirochloe odorata*. Its common Polish name is Bison Grass and folklore has it that it is a favourite food of the Bison. I must confess that I have never managed to tempt a Bison to eat it. The grass, as its name suggests, is very sweet-smelling due to the fact that it contains Coumarin, the substance that puts the smell into new mown hay. I must also confess that, even if the Bison don't like it, I do because it is used to colour and flavour a very special Vodka called Zubrowka, Bison Vodka, and there is a picture on each bottle to prove it!

I well remember my last meeting with Stanislaw Kulczynski, I was then a young, budding peatnick who had just finished two months intensive training from the Maestro himself. He said, 'Well, you have made it, never forget the importance of boundaries'. I never have and I have never forgotten the taste of the Zubrowka in which we drank each other's health.

Some like it hot

Iceland is the last outpost of the Old World, lying as it does only 350 km from the coast of Greenland and 850 km from Scotland. It is an oceanic island, a large one whose 103,100 square kilometres of land lie almost entirely south of the Arctic Circle. Its population, none of whom, apart from the possibility of a few migrants, are Eskimos would not fill Wembley Stadium and it boasts the largest glacier to be found anywhere between the Arctic and Antarctic Circles.

It is a country that has always held my fascination ever since, as a child, I read a book called 'The Wonders of Creation'. It was, and come to that still is, a super leather bound Victorian-type volume illustrated with detailed line drawings, and it had been presented to my grandfather as a prize from his Sunday School. The book is simply bursting with information, being full of detailed accounts of many of the most fabulous parts of the world and it was reading this book which set my feet itching on a life of travel. Two of the chapters have always held for me a special fascination, the one an account of the rain forests of the Amazon, the other of the geothermal phenomena of Iceland.

To cut a long story somewhat shorter that it really need be, I found myself as a rather ancient undergraduate with a cheque for £30, awarded for an essay on the subject of to where and why I would travel if I had £30. My essay, although I say it myself, was a masterpiece of flowing Victoriana explaining that I would travel to Iceland in order to 'witness the wonders nature had afforded there'.

In those days, and it wasn't all that long ago, the fare from Lieth to Reykjavík on the good ship *Gullfoss* was £19·10, third class and so the planning went ahead. At the last minute my companion-to-be was called away for examination purposes and my father decided he would step into the breach and fill the now spare space in my hiking tent. Now seeing that he had never camped before, and that we were not going to get to Iceland until early September, we were both in for a bit of a shock. Nevertheless that trip got me completely hooked on the land of lava and ice.

The first shock was to find both Mountain Avens and Stemless Campion growing between the paving stones, in the outskirts of the capital, as we walked out to find a place to pitch our tent. The second was when morning brought us face to face with the reality of sub-arctic climate and the problem of

Fig 87 *Mountain Avens Dryas octopetala resident of Reykjavik*

trying to fold up a frozen tent. We soon learned to make for an area of geothermal activity before pitching tent, and I can assure you that there is nothing better than underground sheet heating to warm away the pangs of Iceland's frost.

Our travels took us hot foot to the most famous of the hot spring areas, aptly called Geysir where we were to spend a few days basking in the full range of Iceland's temperatures. According to my leather bound book and to no less a personage than the great traveller Lord Dufferin, there was one geyser called the Strokkur, which translated means the churn, would always perform if you annoyed it by hurling something into its broiling cauldron. The account said that the Strokkur always threw it back. A precious tin of you-know-whose what, was lightly punctured, hurled in and we sat back waiting for dinner to be served. Nothing happened, until quite suddenly a quiet voice told us that it had ceased to function many years before, hinting that our guide book must be somewhat out of date. (Please do not confuse Lord Dufferins Strokkur with the one in the modern guide books, which performs at regular intervals.)

From that point on we didn't really need a guide book, because the voice belonged to a local naturalist, called Helgi, who took us on a guided tour around the boiling bubbling lagoons of the area. He also informed us that we were in luck because the Bolshoi Ballet, who were at the time doing a season in Reykjavik, were coming next day to visit the area and in their honour the Great Geyser was going to be doctored in order to make it perform for the assembled company.

A geyser usually consists of a neat saucer shaped depression with a large plug hole in the centre leading down to one or more subterranean chambers, the hole and the whole being filled with water on the simmer. Geothermal activity, or rather the activity which makes the geo-thermal, boils the water, and as one litre of liquid water takes up a lot less room than that same litre when it has turned to vapour, the whole system gets up a real good head of steam. The pressure slowly builds up, until it is sufficient to overcome the weight of the water in the plug hole, or rather the blow hole system, and 'there she blows'. Now in the good old days of Lord Dufferin the Great Geyser used to spout at irregular intervals, the column of steam and water rising to as much as 40 metres. Unfortunately, like the Strokkur, it is today in a more quiescent mood and to make it work requires a goodly dose of soft soap which alters the surface tension of the system and, well we were about to see.

Next day we were very excited and stood in the background

Fig 88 *Command performance of the Great Geyser*

Fig 89 *On the simmer*

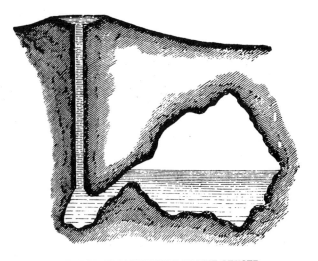

THEORETICAL SKETCH OF THE GEYSER.

as the man with the geothermal enema appeared and ladled it into the bowl. The whole ensemble pirouetted enigmatically around the edge. Nothing happened, in went more soft soap – a graceful pause – and still nothing happened, and so the dancers withdrew to lunch in the local hotel. Lunch over, more soap was administered but all to no avail the Great Geyser was not to be evoked. Off went the coach taking the dancers back for their next performance, leaving us all alone with a now gurgling geysir. No sooner had the bus disappeared over the horizon than there was a great sigh, as if some underground monster was drawing in its breath and there it was, a shimmering column of boiling water which pulsed up to at least 20 metres. It didn't last long, the waters soon receding to leave the bowl empty, so that it was possible to walk to the edge and peer down the hole in the middle. We were like a couple of kids, the Great Geysir primed for the Bolshoi had done a pas-de-deux, me and my dad, we even forgot our tin of baked beans so greedily eaten by the Strokkur.

That night I fell into peaceful geothermal sleep in the shallow end of a swimming pool fed by water from the hot springs, my head pillowed on the jelly like mass of blue green algae growing on the steps. I don't suppose that I slept for very long, but I awoke with a very cold nose, the rest of my body completely wrinkled through long immersion in the warm water.

Of all the habitats on earth the interface between hot spring water and the cold of an arctic winter must rank as one of the most extreme, although the hot water itself is extreme enough. Nothing can live in boiling water, well at least not for long, and so the hottest of the actual springs are devoid of any life. So too are the upper reaches of the streams draining from the spring boils, but as the hot water makes its way downslope, it cools as it flows; its course is usually marked out by a distinct zoning of vegetation, each zone having a distinct colouration. The rate of cooling will depend on the depth of the water and the rate of flow, but usually cooling will take place much more rapidly along the edges of the stream where it is shallower and flows more slowly. It is for this reason that the zonation is in the form of an elongated V. The first plants to come in, and they can tolerate water at about 94°C, are very special bacteria which cannot directly utilise the energy of the sun, but instead makes use of the energy of chemical reations involving sulphur compounds. Volcanic waters abound with sulphur, so what better habitat for these chemoautotrophs, which are often pink in colour. As the stream temperature drops, other less hardy plants can grow and around the 60°C mark extensive mats of a dark blue-green colour show where

Fig 90 *Zonation of vegetation down stream from a hot spring*

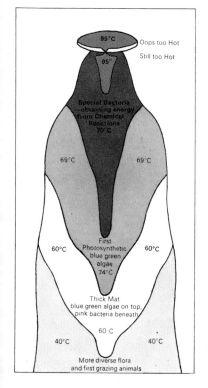

the first of the true photosynthetic plants are able to grow, its name is *Mastigocladus*. As a rule of finger, once the blue green algal mat is present it is safe to immerse your thumb in the water, although you may get a bit of a shock when you feel the algal mat. It is both tough and textured yet soft and spongy, its surface rather like stiff velvet; a close look will reveal the elements of this texture to be very fine filaments, almost black in colour.

Fig 91 *All steamed up*

Even more surprising, the resilient mat may be several centimetres deep and it is possible to cut it open with a knife, revealing a lower jelly consisting of billions of some of the most peculiar plants on earth. The inner mass is made up of filamentous photosynthetic bacteria which, although appearing a lurid yellow or even bright cherry pink, in fact contain special bacteriochlorophylls, which allow them to make use of the red, and even the infra-red, end of the spectrum of sunlight. The interesting fact is that these are exactly the wavelengths of light which filter through the surface weft of blue-green algae. Evolution has produced the components of a jelly sandwich, which is structured to make maximum use of the light which impinges upon the hot spring environment. Deeper in the mat, where little or no light actually penetrates, other bacteria are found living on the products of decay from the productive, sun-worshipping community above, a balanced living system.

If production at the top outstrips decomposition at the bottom, then the mat can get so thick that the top layers will no longer be firmly anchored, and will, therefore, be carried away by the flow of water to drift away down stream. One of the reasons for the success of this self-structured, self-replenishing sandwich is that above 45°C there are no browsing animals, indeed above that temperature there are no eukaryotic organisms present at all.

What's a eukaryotic organism? Well, the most important components of all living things are proteins; these are the chemicals which allows life to tick in such an energetic way, and they must have come into being very early on in the process of evolution. The first living organisms were no more than bags of living chemicals with very little internal structure at all. Their modern counterparts are called prokaryotic organisms, and they include the Bacteria and the Blue Green Algae, some of which are the denizens of the hot spring waters. As evolution continued the living structure became more complex, the protein being arranged within the cells in distinct recognisable aggregates called organelles. Such structured cells are called eukaryotic and so all the cells of all the more complex plants and animals of this type.

One of the main functions of the proteins is to act as catalysts for the complex of chemical reactions that is life. There is a basic law of chemistry which says that all chemical reactions speed up when the temperature increases, and this is equally true of the chemistry of life. The only problem is that the proteins are somewhat delicate and as the temperature increases they begin to be broken down. Using the correct jargon, proteins are thermolobile and if the temperature gets too high they will be denatured, eventually being rendered functionless. Boiling water finishes the lot off, hence no life in the spring boil. The structurally simple prokaryotic organisms can tolerate temperatures which would be death to the more complex eukaryotes. It is still not known whether they have 'tougher' proteins, spend a lot of effort in making new ones as the old ones are denatured, or whether they simply manage to protect them in some way, but the fact is that they can tolerate water above 45°C, and the eukaryotes cannot. This means that the productive photosynthesising sandwich can live gloriously isolated from any nasty animals which might eat it.

Passing downstream from the bubbly hissing spring the zones spell out in glorious colour the opportunities for life and the way in which evolution has seized upon the opportunity and made use of the potential of this most extreme of habitats.

The difference in the tolerance of these two major groups of the living kingdom was brought home to me in a very forceful way while camping down on the Reykjanes peninsula. The night was a hot steamy one in a hot spring area and in the early hours there was a very definite earth tremor. In the morning it was very evident that a number of new hot-water trickles had burst through and all the eukaryotic plants, mosses, liverworts, club mosses and flowering plants had been killed off in broad patches. Twenty-four hours later the edges of the patches were picked out by blue-green jelly-like masses and the V-shaped zonation was beginning to develop down-slope of each spring.

Before I started to swot up for my trip to Iceland I had been under the impression that the only difference which existed between volcanoes was their current level of activity; erupting, thinking about it or extinct. The trouble is that nothing is ever that simple, no not never. In the lava/sulphur scale of volcanoes there are the ones, at one end, which go bang, shooting out vast amounts of dust or tephra and these are called explosive. At the other end of the scale there are the purely effusive members of the volcano clan whose wont is to pour out streams of liquid rock. There are of course mixed up ones which go in for both forms of volcanic exhibitionism and it is these which produce the enormous cones of the classical volcanoes like the in-famous Fuji of Japan.

Iceland's highest mountain Oraefajökull is a volcano of the mixed up type although its 2119 metre high cone is very difficult to see because it is covered in ice. 'Jökull' is the Ice-landic word for glacier. This is also true of a number of Iceland's more active volcanoes and it is an unfortunate fact of physics that even solid water and fire cannot be mixed without something spectacular happening. When one of these sub-ice volcanoes goes up massive floods add to the more normal problems of devastation which are part and parcel of an eruption.

Molten rock alone pouring from a single vent produces what is known as a shield volcano, which is all lopsided and rarely rises to any great height; while the purely explosive types just blow out a crater, which may later be filled with water to form a crater lake. Many of Iceland's volcanoes are much more complex, they consist of elongated fissures with rows of craters all of which pour out lava. Topping the lot at least in complexity is Mount Hekla immortalised forever in the name of one of Messrs Brock's pyrotechnic fantasmagoria; it is a mixture of the lot, effusive, explosive, cone, shield, fissure and all. I must admit that I didn't realise that it was quite such a mixed up mountain when I sat one day sheltering just within the rim of one of its craters, basking in the sulphurous warmth of the rocks contemplating a large spanish onion, all we had left from our climbing rations.

Famous as Hekla is, the most famous of all Icelandic eruptions was from the Laki row, a fissure volcano which stretches for more than 25 kms and erupted for seven terrible months of 1783. Its hundred plus craters poured forth a mass of lava, which today covers 565 sq km of Iceland, and a bluish haze that covered both Europe and much of Western Asia. This same haze shut off the light of the sun to such an extent that most of Iceland's crops failed and famine followed in the wake of this awesome eruption.

The majority of the volcanoes found on this oceanic island are of the effusive type and it is estimated that in recent years they have together produced more than one third of the world's lava, one third of the world's youngest visible rock. It is for this reason that one feature which sets this piece of the old world apart from all the rest is its young landscape, and like all young things Iceland appears to like it hot.

If you were to drill a bore-hole down through any other part of Europe on lowering a thermometer you would find that the temperature on average rises by $0.03°C$ per metre. Over much of Iceland a similar bore-hole would yield figures of around $0.1°C$ per metre and you don't have to be too much of a mathematician to calculate that at a depth of only 1 km any water present in the rock would be at boiling point. Hence all those hot springs.

Just like volcanoes, there are many different sorts of hot spring but the areas in which they are found may be conveniently placed in one of two categories. The first one, the cooler of the two is therefore called a low temperature field and it is these which produce the spouting geysers and the main outpourings of hot water. Deildartunguhver in the mid-west of the Island boasts the largest hot spring in the world which produces 250 litres of boiling water every second. Hot as that may appear to be, the second category contains hotter spots in which the thermal gradient may be as much as $1°C$ per metre, and in such places the water turns to steam before it reaches the surface. The steam fields are very spectacular places, all of a hiss and a gurgle, and not the place in which to park your tent unless you want a wet as well as a warm night.

It is often easy to tell from a distance whether you are approaching a steam or a hot water field, because the former support only a very sparse vegetation. Steam fields produce an awful lot of sulphur, and this, added to the problems of living with your roots bathed in warm water and your shoots waving in the cold arctic wind, appears to be just too much for the majority of the members of even the hardy sub-arctic flora.

In contrast the hot water fields are less harsh habitats and their environs abound with many plants.

Iceland, land of glaciers, young rocks, hot springs, catastrophic eruptions and earthquakes is at first sight not a very likely place in which to find a luxuriant vegetation. Yet if we can believe the early accounts, when man arrived on the hot, cold scene he found a wooded landscape. Ari the Wise wrote that during the time of the first settlement somewhere around the year AD 900 the country was 'wooded between the coasts and the mountains'. However much of an exaggeration that was, there is very little woodland left today and the treeline of stunted Birch lies somewhere between the 300 to 400 metre contour. Before man decided that Iceland would be a good place to live there were no large herbivores, in fact there weren't even any small mammalian grazers. Man introduced his Sheep on purpose and his Rats and Mice probably by accident: these combined with fire and other methods of forest clearance, soon reduced the park tundra to the treeless landscape which now spreads from the coasts to the edge of the mountains and the inland desert. Loss of topsoil has gone hand in hand with removal of the trees so much so that over 20,000 sq km of the lowlands are today virtual deserts. Like the sulphur in the steam fields man has in places added the last straw to the harsh environment, bringing about widespread collapse of the system, and the marked deterioration of Iceland's climate since the thirteenth century has not helped in any way.

Fig 92 *Cassiope tetragona*
I wish it grew in Britain

Much of the lowland part of the Island is today covered with a drab mantle of brown green tundra, the lower-lying tracts of land overflowing with the more colourful mosses typical of arctic mires. Iceland's total flora of flowering plants and ferns is only some 450, the most abundant members being sedges and grasses. Of all the plants of the Icelandic tundra there is one which I wish we had in Britain and that is *Cassiope tetragona* the Arctic or Tundra Bell Heather. It is a very handsome plant its branches covered in an ordered array of overlapping (imbricate) leaves which give the shoots an almost succulent appearance. From each of the neat leaf clad branches a drooping flower stalk arises, a perfect bell flower pendulous from its apex. Just why this hardy tundra plant is missing from the mountains of Scotland is hard to understand, perhaps it is the presence and dominance of the more robust heather, or perhaps due to the fact that when much of Scotland was forested the woodlands were thicker.

Travelling through Iceland you can't help but get the feeling that man is beginning to overcome the problems of the past, turning the limitations of the land of ice and fire to good account. I will never forget on a very cold day late in my first visit standing in the driving sleet and peering into the warmth of a greenhouse heated from the local steam field. I felt as frozen as the surrounding tundra. 2 mm away, through the thickness of the glass, bananas were in full flower. There are today many hectares of glass under which a great variety of vegetables, fruits and decorative plants are grown.

Extensive areas of the semi-desert lands are being brought back to stability by the planting of Lyme Grass, and experimental trials with the addition of fertiliser has shown that even the desert can be made to bear vegetation sufficient to provide grazing for livestock and the visiting birds alike. Likewise forest trials using Sitka Spruce culled from the parts of Alaska which have a similar climate to that of Iceland have paved the way to the possibility of large scale forestry.

This is one place in the world where goats, the animals which are so often the scourge of all attempts at revitalisation of a landscape, are on the decline and indeed today very few are left. More sadly the Reindeer introduced to the Island from Norway some 100 years ago today only exist in a natural state in some small pockets in the highlands. The greatest nuisance of recent times is the Mink which only escaped from captivity probably in 1936 and yet is already creating havoc with some of the nesting birds.

The face of Iceland is changing and although one can probably look to a time when it will be saga-green once more I hope that at least some parts will remain untamed by man. There is no place quite like the interior desertscapes where the Sprengisandur squeezes itself between the great bulk of the Vatnajökull and the lesser ice mass of the Hofsjökull. The sands are black and waterlogged and in the watery sun of an autumn evening, the ice is blue or blush-pink. It's a long walk down from Akureyri in the north, but well worth it just for the feeling of complete solitude. The cairned road is not only the route for all itinerant naturalists, but also the chosen flight path for the geese which have spent their summers further north. They congregate in their thousands in noisome array, parting to allow the footslogging traveller right of way. Only when the wind is blowing in the right direction do they take wing overflying you a couple of days later. This is the real Iceland and it looks great from ground level so what they see from up there I can only guess.

Fig 93 *Pink Feet on the move*

One small corner

Why is it that regulation English type travellers always like to take their tea with them? The slick answer is of course, because no one else can make tea like we do back home. A pre-warmed teapot of glazed brownware, regulation teaspoons heaped one per person and per pot, four minutes to draw and ahh! five minutes of fragrant pleasure. That's tea the English way. Those tall glasses held indelicately in wrought chrome, the perforated aseptic foil tube which one wags around with little hope in the luke warm water is just not on. So the old English maxim is: it's best to take it with you. Ceylon, Darjeeling, Lapsang, Earl Grey – whatever your flavour fad – it's there in the packet just waiting to be boiled out. So whenever I am on the move my packet of favourite tea comes along with me.

I well remember one very hot day while driving through the south of Italy I stopped the car to take in the Straits of Messina with the angular mass of Sicily beyond. The rocks crackled in the heat, the green of spring was drying into the spines of summer and I was dying for a cuppa, but knew that my packet was long since empty. A can of parboiled coke only added insult to the pangs of thirst and as I sat down to at least enjoy the view my fourth sense smelt bliss, the unmistakable bouquet of Earl Grey. It was emanating not from a local hostelry but from a pile of wicker crates empty and discarded in the corner of a field which was itself planted with rows of trees, neatly spaced, the rows intermeshed with a bright green shrub. Both the trunk of the tree and its shiny foliage, said citrus but in the absence of flowers and fruits that was the nearest I could get. I finished my coke and forgot all about the mystery tree but only until my next encounter with a tin of Earl Grey. There in small print was the name of the tree 'a delicate blend of the best china teas flavoured with essence of Bergamot'.

The Bergamot is a member of the family of flowering plants which bears the name Rutaceae, as are all the other citrus fruits of commerce, the Orange, Lemon, Lime, Grapefruit, Ugli, Tangerine, etc, etc. Even in the absence of fruit they are not too difficult to place in their genealogy as long as you have got a flower. The most characteristic feature of the citrus flower is the fact that its stamens which bear the anthers (pollen sacs) are fused into a number of distinct groups or bundles. Be very careful because not all the members of the Rutaceae have fused

Fig 94 *Citrus blossom*

FLORAL DIAGRAM *Note the groups of anthers*

Fig 95 *What a lot of Bergamots I've got*

anthers and the character is present in a few other families.

I am now going to let you into a secret, I collect flowers (please read on very quickly before you get too cross) but I do it in a very special way. Out comes my sketch book and I make rapid notes. (1) The number of sepals, petals, anthers and ovaries; (2) how they are arranged, i.e., in rings (whorls) or in spirals; (3) whether they are separate or fused together; (4) finally I make a quick sketch. This gives me sufficient information with which to draw a floral diagram, over page. Now the first few you draw will in all probability be a series of near catastrophes, and if you are as bad an artist as I, so will the next few hundred. However practise makes perfect and eventually each of your diagrams will be a floral tribute to the perfection of the flower and it will also tell you a lot about the family it comes from, and will certainly help you to get the feeling of the great group of the flowering plants.

Once the fruit is formed there is no problem, a Bergamot looks like an unripe orange.

All citrus fruits are berries. After pollination the tissues of the ovary swell up, filling with the rich juice which helps to protect the developing seeds. The ovary wall becomes a thick protective skin which will later ripen to a full yellow, attracting birds and animals to peck away the fruit and spread the seeds. Next time you bite on an orange look at the small shining vesicles each one bursting with sweetness, they have a very different taste to the harsh bitterness of the skin. No, don't just chuck the skin away – remember the mist of droplets which spray from the surface while peeling? Each drop emanates from a small complex gland which when placed

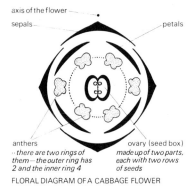

axis of the flower —
sepals —   — petals

anthers
··there are two rings of
them—the outer ring has
2 and the inner ring 4

ovary (seed box)
made up of two parts,
each with two rows
of seeds

FLORAL DIAGRAM OF A CABBAGE FLOWER

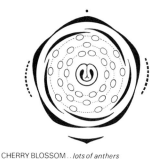

CHERRY BLOSSOM.. *lots of anthers*

A BLUSHING VIOLET.. *note the spur is getting harder*

Fig 96 Floral diagrams, formalize the structure of a flower, easy to read once you know the code

Opposite page

There she blows, geyser in action (Chapter Nine)

under pressure, releases a drop of oil that will mark paper with an opalescent transparency. A piece of full ripe orange skin squeezed across the flame of a lighted match produces squirts of roaring fire as the oil ignites, volatizing its fragrance in a plume of smoke.

That is what Bergamots are all about, their secret is in the special fragrance of their skin, a fragrance which can be imparted to the skins of others who are fortunate enough to afford the best of colognes. When you apply Cologne, the first fragrance all depends on oil of Bergamot, for it is its volatile spirit that provides the high notes in the melody that is a good perfume. The mark of a good Cologne is the length of time for which those top notes are held. If they linger on and on then it's the real stuff, for the cheap counterparts which use synthetics soon lose their top range.

That first encounter with the true Bergamot was to lead me through some surprising places and some surprising facts, not the least being far removed from southern Italy, to be exact Ashford in Kent. As you come into Ashford off the Dover road you are regaled with a bouquet of· fragrance, enough to stimulate the least fastidious of noses and some plain but striking notices in mauve – or is it violet? – that proclaim the presence of one of the world's leading houses of fragrance.

It was there within sound of the Oast houses that I was to learn a little something about the world of perfume. I was led through great rooms looking not unlike the inside of some intricate steam organ, each gleaming pipe bearing the name of some exotic, distilled from the fields of the world, roses from Bulgaria, Stephanotis from the Alpes Maritimes, Mint from Mitcham, and of course Bergamot from Reggio Calabria over-looking the Straits of Messina.

It is to the compounding rooms of this great fragrance house (the word factory would be far too vulgar), that all the essences, distillates and essential oils come to be mixed and blended, or perhaps the correct word is composed, into the symphonies of world famous perfumes.

The compounding room is the place where each melody is orchestrated in gleaming chariots which are driven from pipe to pipe tapping off by weight, just the right amount of fragrance to fit the score. Much as I wanted to try my hand and drive one of the perfume chariots I had to be content to stand and watch. Compounding is a craft learned through years of patient apprenticeship and one false turn of the spigot could ruin many thousands of pounds worth of the very precious ingredients. Take for instance the fact that to make one pound of attar of roses requires a hundred million petals.

The voice that led me through this world of perfume belonged to the firm's Public Relationship Officer and as I listened to the astounding flow of fact I suddenly realised that this was the voice of Olive Stephens, the lady who for three years had been a resident brain on the panel of 'Ask Me Another'.

Perhaps even more astounding than the delicate skill of the compounder and the volume of information from Olive Stephens are the noses of the perfumiers themselves. They are chemists who sniff their days away, testing as only the human nose can test the quality of each ingredient, quality control by those who nose. However, of all the noses in the world one of the most, discerning, especially when it comes to Bergamots belongs to Dr Antonino Giuffre who lives his scented life overlooking the Straits of Messina. Not only can his nose discern the vintage but also from which hillslope the particular oil of Bergamot was derived. Reggio is the capital of Calabria and the south of Calabria is the only true home of the Bergamot and the best of all Bergamots come from the groves which grace the dry south-facing slopes between Cap al'Armi and Capo Sportaventie on the southernmost coast of the toe of Italy.

Citrus bergamia (Risso) is a truly fastidious plant, demanding the most temperate of climates where the temperature ranges only between 3° and 37°C with no sharp rises or falls. The summers must be hot and dry, with water on tap for irrigation, for all the rain must fall in the autumn or winter period. In these conditions a mature tree can in its prime yield 800 to 1,000 fruits. Unlike the Lemon which blooms all around the year the Bergamot blossoms only in the April/May interface and the green fruits develop very slowly ripening to yellow in mid December. The prime time for picking is just as they begin to change colour and they are handled off the tree with the care they deserve.

Modern mechanisms soon extract the oil and although the product is not as good as that which was at one time pressed from the fruit onto high class sponges, the result is good enough to leave even the nose of Dr Giuffre unwrinkled. The oil from the skin is thus the most important product, but none of the fruit goes to waste. The juice is rich in other organic compounds and the pulp, under the name of Pistaccao, goes for silage to feed livestock. On Dr Giuffre's farm the manure from the cattle is used to fertilize the soil in which Bergamot grows. Only the pips are useless for they are infertile and cannot be grown. All new Bergamot trees are propagated by grafting, usually onto a foot of the Bitter Orange.

Opposite page

(*Chapter Ten*)

Top left
Bergamots, fragrance skin deep

Bottom left
Essences of Bergamot

Top right
Silk in the making

Bottom right
Fashioned in silk

It is thought that the Bergamot may have originated in Calabria by grafting or hybridization, although certain authorities seek its origin in the Canaries, Greece, or even India. Whatever its exact origin there is no getting away from the nasal evidence that the best of the world's Bergamots grow in one small corner of Italy. Here the conditions are perfect, the high Appenino Calabrese, rising to over 1950 metres from the dissected coast, provide all the water needed for summer irrigation and so the crop grows to fragrant perfection.

Although citrus fruits are a prominent feature of the frescoes of Pompeii, and the Crusaders were familiar with the Bergamots of Calabria, the first commercial plantations did not come into being until around the year 1770, to meet the demand for the new Waters of Cologne.

Fig 97 Bergamot dozer in action

The formula of Eau de Cologne was invented by an Italian by the name of Ferminis, some 400 years ago and the secret was carried by an itinerant Italian worker by the name of Farina to Cologne, where it has remained ever since. Even to this day the volatile waters of Cologne are absolutely dependant upon the oil expressed from the Bergamots of Calabria. Unfortunately, even with the modern methods and machines, the production of the essential oil is labour intensive in the extreme and its days could well be numbered. In many orchards their trunks are being used as a foot on which to graft new ready cash crops like Clementines or worse still the trees are uprooted to make way for beans or buildings.

The reasons are of course much more complex than the straight economics of production, they always are. Synthetic oil of Bergamot was developed during the last war, when the supply routes were cut, and cheaper labour in the Sudan is making their oil of Bergamot much more competitive with the real stuff. Perhaps the noses of the masses are not quite as fastidious as that of Dr Giuffre, and who, in this modern throw-away world of instant pop, really wants a melody of fragrance that will linger on? Whatever the real reason – and like the real Cologne it must be a true amalgam of many – the fragrance of this small corner of Southern Europe may well, unfortunately, volatilise into just another memory of the twenty-first century.

The family, to which the Bergamot owes its botanical allegiance, numbers amongst its members some very unusual plants with some very unusual odours, much less pleasant than their exalted cousin. One of these is *Ruta graveolens*, the common Mediterranean Rue. It is a poisonous plant which warns of its 'venom' with a strong unpleasant smell, the product of special aromatic glands. Poisonous and unpleasant it may be, but for centuries it has been highly prized as a medicinal plant, and like many other plants of medicinal repute it is used to impart a unique flavour to the cure all, alcohol.

Fig 98 *Jasmine, sweet fragrance before enfleurage*

Grappa Ruta, though an acquired taste, is one of the better ways of imbibing near neat alcohol and it can be taken in the best of spirits, both as an aperitif and an after dinner liqueur. To prove that this, the prince of Grappas, really does contain the essence of the Common Rue, there is often a sprig of the plant in each bottle. A word of warning – never drink too much, especially on those cool warm winter days of Calabria, while the Bergamots are being picked and the Jasmine is in flower. The effect can be too much, transporting you far away to the mystic east. Not that you need all that much transporting, for a short journey up into the hills takes you to another secret of Calabria, as exotic as the last.

The transition from the dry coastal slopes into the mountains, from whence cometh the irrigation water of summer, is as rapid as the rush of water down the torrents of spring. The neat orchards of citrus give way to a jumble of large leaved oaks, immixed with Umbrella Pine and the waxen flowers of the Strawberry Tree. Smaller fields, terraced on the steep slopes, produce a variety of crops, their margins picked out by trees with broad almost fleshy leaves. They are White Mulberry trees around and between which the tracks wind donkey-wise to the summits, each of which is surmounted by a village. These large leaves, smooth and shiny above, with hairs only on the veins beneath, form the basis of what is unfortunately another dying industry of Calabria.

The White Mulberry is a native of China from whence it was introduced by a long and tortuous route to be planted, both for ornament and as food, for the Silkworm. In fact, both the Mulberry and the Silkworms were smuggled out of China with fear of death or worse hanging over the smugglers. The route was via Khotan, India, Persia and Greece. It was not until the year AD 947, that they were brought to Sicily and later to the hills of Calabria, over 3000 years after the Chinese had

Fig 99 *'Silk factories on the hoof'*

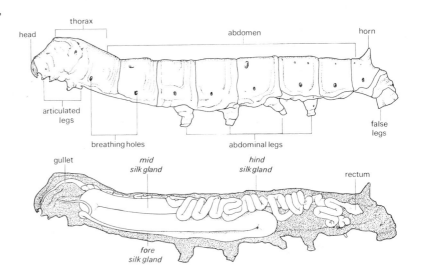

discovered the art and craft of the manufacture of the world's finest cloth.

Morus alba L is the latin name of the White Mulberry and *Bombyx mori* L the name of the Silk Moth, which is the more showy stage of the life cycle of the Silkworm.

Each silkworm has two special glands situated near its front end, and each is capable of extruding a continuous filament of purest protein called fibroin. The two fibroin filaments are automatically cemented together with a gum called sericin, and together the three elements of this protein cocktail form the raw silk fibre, which is endowed with some very unique properties.

A filament of silk is stronger than a similar filament of steel, with an incredible breaking strength of over 65,000 pounds per square inch. It is a good insulator, is not injured by temperatures as high as 284°F and can soak up 30% of its weight in water, and still feel dry. It is thus the ideal substance with which a caterpillar can protect itself from the elements, while it undergoes its most important transformations, metamorphosis, first into a pupae, and then into a moth.

It may seem somewhat of a paradox to find a protein playing a protective role in nature. The enzymes which are the catalysts of all the life processes are proteins and are among the most reactive of the life chemicals. Fibroin is a structural protein and, although composed of the same four elements as the enzymes, namely nitrogen, carbon, hydrogen and oxygen they are structured in such a way that, once extruded, they are inert.

Fig 100 *Sericulture Chinese style Picture painted on silk by Chao Ping-Tsun in the thirty-fifth year of Kang Hsi 1696*

There is only one property of silk as made by man which is not enjoyed by the Silkworm itself and that is called scroop by the trade. Scroop is the quality which give silk garments their own special rustling sound and man has put it there, by washing the fibre in a bath of vinegar.

The cost of labour and the introduction of artificial fibres, with equal strength and lustre though lacking the authentic scroop, is hastening the end of the silk farms of Calabria. Yet, if you know just where to listen you can hear the clack clack of the looms, as the traditional patterns are woven into the most lustruous of all natural fabrics.

Before I visited the silk weavers of Calabria it had been one of my desires to own a silk shirt. Now my ambition is to sleep under a counterpane of purest fibroin emboidered with flowers by the skillful hands of the ladies of the village of Cortale. Each one takes more than six months to complete and each is as perfect as anything which has travelled the trade routes to and from the mystic east.

Sitting under a Mulberry, dreaming of my silken coverlid and watching a Silkworm spin its white cocoon, I couldn't help thinking of another process, which turns a protein into a thing of rare beauty, Mozzarella cheese.

A new autostrada leads north out of Reggio, winding high above the Straits of Messina towards Salerno, famous as a landing place in the second world war but equally famous in peace time for its original Mozzarella cheese, which is made from the milk of the Water Buffalo.

The first time I saw the Water Buffalo of Battipaglia was when I was just home from India, and it took me some moments to realise that I was not the victim of some Grappa soaked dream. No, they were real enough, gentle timid creatures, their great horns sweeping back reflected in the water of the meadows in which they grazed. Up to that moment the only Mozzarella cheese I had ever tasted was that pre melted onto a Pizza, its taste obscured by anchovy and pomadoro.

Mozzarella is made for the Pizza industry in many parts of Italy, and it is made from the milk of cows, but the real stuff is made from that of the Buffalo. Like silk, milk is a protein secreted by the special glands which set the mammals apart from all other animal groups.

The protein in question is a complex centering on casein, and of all the natural proteins, man has learned to manipulate milk in more ways than any other. The range of products is as fantastic as the range of processes. The former go from milk shakes, ice creams, butter, yoghurt through to the world council of cheeses, the latter from beating, freezing, churning through to the whole complex of enzyme treatments and

Fig 101 *Water Buffalo,*
producing high grade protein

natural fermentation, which gradually replace the taste and texture of the daily pinta with those of one's favourite fromage.

The milk of the Buffaloes of Battipaglia is no exception and the cheeses can only be described as exceptional. The best, at least for my palate is the real Mozzarella di Bufala. It is a cheese whose flavour is not far removed from that of the milk, its special texture is kneaded in while hot, until the mass can be pulled about rather like well chewed gum. Round cheeses are then pinched off from the mass and kept in fresh cold water until eaten, and the sooner they are eaten the better. There are a whole series of trattorias, spotlessly clean on the road that skirts the Buffalo Fields. You don't even have to be able to ask for your meal in Italian, they just serve up the Mozzarella perfect everytime. On its own, a little salt, black pepper or even a sprinkling of olive oil, this is really perfection in protein.

In the past there were many more Water Buffaloes and one supposes the real cheese was much more plentiful. The reason for their decline was that the wet fields, on which their own slow way of life depends, were breeding places for mosquitos and hence for malaria. It was under the eye of Mussolini's government that the great coastal swamps were drained to rid Italy from the scourge that in all probability helped bring about the decline, if not the fall, of the might of Rome.

Today, as the economy of Italy grows in strength, the palates of the modern Romans are demanding the taste of fresh Mozzarella. Plans are already well afoot to build up the once dwindling stocks of Buffalo, first by creating the water meadows they require. The modern Buffalo herd is housed in absolute luxury, fed on the best of corn silage and pampered throughout their lives. Each herd unit has its byre complete with private swimming pool and mud wallow, enough to provide the animals with a regulation mud pack to keep them cool and protected from the biting insects.

When filming we were fortunate to have as our host Vincenzo Citro and as our guide and teacher his fourteen year old son, Angelo, who not only spoke very good English but knew the business inside out. For two gloriously Mozzarella soaked days we were organised through the intricacies not only of cheese manufacture, but Buffalo breeding and farm management.

The Valtusciana cheese works overflowed with the full range of buffalo milk cheeses, offering a range of tastes which must, in the near future, tempt the palates of the world. The Citro farm likewise overflowed with all sorts of exciting experiments. Hydroponic culture of Tomatoes, new gigantic varieties of Grapefruit, the mysterious, delicious Lotus fruit, pink and plump hanging from leafless trees and vines bearing the first ever local crop of Chinese Gooseberries. All proclaiming the enormous potential of this one small corner of Europe, where west meets and mingles with the exotics of the east.

The last import from the east into the region comes from Japan. No, it's not even a fruit, it is a gleaming as-up-to-date-as-they-come factory for dealing with a new source of protein. Protein from petroleum. It seems very much out of place. The factory certainly does nothing to enhance the beauties of the coastline nor the Bergamot groves over which it towers. But is it out of place? Bergamots came, or were evolved here, to meet a then modern demand, likewise the biology and the technology of sericulture. The Buffaloes, almost lost through modern drainage are now coming back into their own. Plastic meat? Surely that is the end of the road, well I suppose it is for some, but it must be the beginning for others.

Fig 102 *Protein from petroleum — a new factory in Calabria*

In the hills of Calabria some people still speak a dialect of the Greek language, a left over from the days when this part of Italy was under the sway of the Greek civilization. This alone marks out the remoteness of the area, at least until very recent times.

Most of the modern tourist routes stop at Pompeii, a few extend down to include the great temples of Paestum. Few venture further south into Campania, the Garden of Italy, home of the Water Buffalo, let alone down into Calabria which has for so long been the Garden of the Waters of Cologne. The new autostrada must change all this, I only hope that it is a change for the better for everyone.

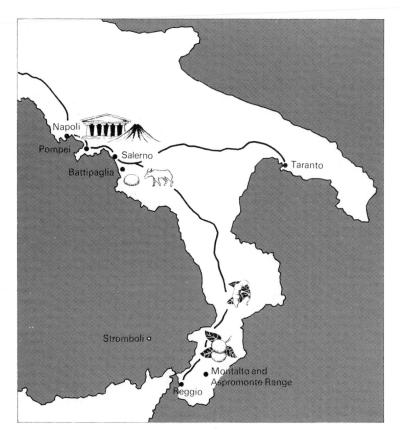

Fig 103 *Beyond the tourist routes in southern Italy*

Postscript

Do you have a secret desire? Well one of mine had always been to tread the cat walk of one of the great Fashion Houses of Paris. I don't know exactly why, but there it was. I have at last got it out of my system because the last shot of One Small Corner and indeed of the whole series was shot at Pierre Balmain's.

I will always remember sitting in the glare of the arc lights surrounded by the affluence of Europe and feeling decidedly tatty, and this is what I said.

Fig 104 *Fashioned by Balmain – with woman in mind*

"Oil of Bergamot, a product of the skin of a not too exalted member of the Great Family of Citrus Fruits. Silk, produced by what to most people are nasty creepy crawly caterpillars. Two very special products of Europe and they meet here in Paris fashioned by Pierre Balmain with woman very much in mind." Now these two products epitomise the whole wealth of Europe, a group of countries from which men have gone to the four corners of the world searching for natural products to enrich our lives. The fact that some of the plants and animals they found now live and are actually farmed within the bounds of Europe show us the great diversity of the environments of this quite small mass of land. From the cold of Arctic Finland and the high peaks of the Alps, the sub-tropical dryscapes of the Med., the wet Atlantic coast and the almost desert Cabo de Gata each climate, each landscape has something special to offer both to man and nature.

Unfortunately we are beginning to muck it all up. It used to be fun to think that only 21 miles across the Channel there was a whole new world of cultures waiting to be discovered. Now you can savour Danish pastries, buy Paris fashions, original Slivovitz, Borsch – all without moving from Oxford Street. Even if you do bother to move you don't even get the fun of having your passport stamped any more so you haven't even got an official record to boast exactly where you have been.

La Grande Tour is unfortunately no longer so Grande, at least for the ordinary tourist.

But for the Naturalist things haven't changed all that much. It is all still there, the wonder and excitement of, for you, new plants and new animals to find, especially new types of vege- tation – each one fitting the landscape like some well-tailored garment; each one telling of the wealth of the environment.

Now when I first became a Botanist I decided that I was going to try to get to know each one of the types of vegetation to be found in Europe. I have still got an awful long way to go and, thank goodness, an awful lot of Europe still to see. Thank you for joining me.

DAVID J. BELLAMY
1976

Booklist

Some books that might help you on your travels:

Flora Europaea edited by T. G. Tutin and others. Cambridge University Press, 1964–1976. Four large volumes. This is the ultimate reference work as far as the plants are concerned. Don't try to take it on holiday with you.

BRINK, F. H. VAN DEN *A field guide to the mammals of Britain and Europe.* Collins, 1967.

HUXLEY, A. J. *Mountain flowers in colour.* Blandford Press, 1967. One of my favourites, fits in the pocket, lots of super pictures and good habitat information.

McCLINTOCK, D. and FITTER, R. S. R. *Collins pocket guide to wild flowers.* Collins, 1956. Super book like all the rest of the Collins guides.

PETERSON, R., and others. *A field guide to the birds of Britain and Europe.* Collins, 1970.

POLUNIN, O. *Flowers of Europe.* Oxford University Press, 1969. It's great!

POLUNIN, O. and HUXLEY, A. J. *Flowers of the Mediterranean.* Chatto and Windus, 1965. Super book, lots of nice illustrations, fits into a large pocket.

RIEDL, R. *Fauna und flora der Adria.* Hamburg: Verlag Paul Parey, 1970. Sorry this is in German, but it is full of pictures and lets you identify many of the plants and animals of the Mediterranean seaside.

WILKINSON, G. *Trees in the wild.* Stephen Hope Books, 1973. I like trees and I like this book.

More general books:

CHURCH, R. J. and others. *Advanced geography of northern and western Europe.* Hulton Educational, 2nd rev. edn., 1973. Here are the facts linking environment, vegetation and man.

HENFREY, A. *The vegetation of Europe, its conditions and causes.* London: John van Voorst, 1852. A golden oldie, if you can find one read it, it isn't 100% correct by today's standard, but is very stimulating.

WALTER, H. *Vegetation of the earth: in relation to climate and the eco-physiological conditions* (Heidelberg Science Library, 15). New York: Springer-Verlag, 1973. This is my bible, full of good information and ideas, it makes me feel like a plant.

Acknowledgements

A book is an amalgam of ideas translated into words borrowed from the dictionaries of the world and woven into a living book through the skills of publishers, compositors and binders. You can read it, savour it, feel it and above all own it as a permanent well loved possession.

A television series is a much less permanent thing and yet it is an amalgam of just as many ideas and even more skills. Ideas which are only made real by a team of skills which gradually evolve into a working unit.

Researchers and production assistants pave the way from paper to real live locations, asking endless questions, seeking endless permission and solving endless problems. The team at last hits the road and those ephemeral moments when all the conditions are right (often thanks to the skill of a Lighting Unit) are captured on celluloid and tape by the patience and immense skill of the Camera Crew.

Director and Producer means just that. They take the brunt of the worries and frustrations from first budget to last slate. When the exciting, all-absorbing 'on location' stuff is finished then begins the long job in the cutting room where the ideas and expertise of the whole team are woven by the hand of the editor and the technicians of the celluloid industry into the finished product. As the man in front of the scenes I would like to thank all· those who helped to capture the fact in the permanence of print.

Recording: Mervyn Broadway, John Hore, Dennis Panchen. *Camera:* Yousuf Asiz, A. A. Englander, Ken MacMillan, Chris Sadler. *Research and Producer's Assistant:* Adrian Warren, Sheila Millington. *Director:* Anna Jackson. *Editor:* John Billingham. *Producer:* not-so-old Uncle Mike Weatherley and all the others who gave their time, advice and expertise while on location.

D. J. Bellamy.

Acknowledgments are due to the following for permission to reproduce photographs:

F. G. H. ALLEN *Cynomorium coccinium*, page 51, *Psilotum nudum*, page 56; ARDEA *Iris cretica*, page 93, *Ophrys muscifera*, opp. page 96; PIERRE BALMAIN fashion models, page 139; BARNABY'S PICTURE LIBRARY Mont Blanc (Sylvie Nickels), page 8; DAVID BELLAMY Dover cliffs, page 11, Beech Marten, page 16, *Pinus cembra* (two pictures), page 34, *Cynomorium coccinium*, page 51, stranded boat in Finland, opp. page 65, cattle, page 68, microclimates of Venice, page 81, bergamots, page 127 and opp. page 129, tractor, page 130, Jasmine, page 131, Water Buffalo, page 134, factory, page 136; JOHN BILLINGHAM Alpine Poppy, Globe Flower, *Gentian, Soldanella*, opp. page 32, the Pupplinger Au, opp. page 33, Dwarf Willow, page 33; BRITISH LIBRARY Italian garden plan, page 78; MERVYN BROADWAY Yellow Thistle, page 18, 'Guess who?', page 45; CAMERA PRESS LTD hot springs, Iceland, page 119, model in silk dress (Paris Graphic), opp. page 129; BRUCE COLEMAN LTD *Ophrys spheghodes, Ophrys tenthredinifera* (both A. J. Deane), *Ophrys apifera* (Derek Washington), opp. page 96; *Cassiope tetragona* (Charlie Ott), page 123; C. J. DAWKINS *Asarabacca*, page 38; HELSINKI UNIVERSITY aapa mire, palsa mire, page 70; JOHN HILLELSON Lasithi plateau (Marc Riboud-Magnum), page 88; HIRMER VERLAG throne room, Knossos, page 97; ANTHONY HUXLEY Chamois cress, Trumpet gentian, page 43, *Phoenix theophrasti*, page 89, *Ranunculus asiaticus, Anemone coronaria*, page 93, *Ophrys scolopax, Ophrys fuciflora, Ophrys cretica*, opp. page 96; SIR JOHN KESWICK Oriental silk picture, page 133; FRANK LANE *Genetta genetta* (Francoise Merlet), page 58; NATURAL HISTORY PHOTOGRAPHIC AGENCY Silk Worm spinning cocoon (Stephen Dalton), opp. page 129; D. & M. PARISH *Tamarix gallica*, Alpine Toadflax, page 43; A.'P. PATERSON *Alyssoides cretica*, page 93; O. POLUNIN Spring Gentian, page 43, *Ebenus creticus*, page 93, Mountain Aven, page 115; PRESS ASSOCIATION Finnish lakes (Lehtikuvaoy, Helsinki), page 62; ROGER-VIOLLET cliffs, Cap Blanc Nez, page 11; DAVID AND KATIE URRY geese, page 25; BARBARA WACE geyser, opp. page 128; ADRIAN WARREN front cover, Cabo de Gata, page 7, *Rana esculenta*, page 13, Spider on flower, page 27, *Gentian, Saxifraga*, opp. page 32, Crab Spider eating bee, page 55, lynx monument, National Park Administration headquarters, page 58, Sea Thrift, page 59, creeping dunes, page 60, Crab Spider on daisy, field of flowers, oasis, opp. page 64, *Campanula* on drainpipe, David Bellamy at mussel farm, opp. page 65, garden, Venice, page 79, *Phragmites* reeds, Venice, page 83, fish farming, page 85, Istrian stone, page 87, Bieloweja forest, opp. page 97, Stork, page 103, Elk, page 108, Bieloweja forest, page 111, Bison, page 113.

Illustrations on the following pages are by Constance Dear: 15, 26, 39, 50, 57, 63, 67, 72, 76, 80, 86, 90, 98, 100, 107, 114, 126, 128, 132. Diagrams are by Peter Taylor.